GREAT
MILITARY
LEADERS

Sun
Tzu

Meghan Cooper

Cavendish
Square

Published in 2018 by Cavendish Square Publishing, LLC
243 5th Avenue, Suite 136, New York, NY 10016

First Edition

Website: cavendishsq.com

This publication represents the opinions and views of the author based on his or her personal experience, knowledge, and research. The information in this book serves as a general guide only. The author and publisher have used their best efforts in preparing this book and disclaim liability rising directly or indirectly from the use and application of this book.

CPSIA Compliance Information: Batch #CS17CSQ

All websites were available and accurate when this book was sent to press.

Library of Congress Cataloging-in-Publication Data

Names: Cooper, Meghan, author.
Title: Sun Tzu / Meghan Cooper.
Description: New York : Cavendish Square Publishing, [2018] | Series: Great military leaders | Includes bibliographical references and index.
Identifiers: LCCN 2016058600 (print) | LCCN 2016059951 (ebook) | ISBN 9781502628671 (library bound) | ISBN 9781502628688 (E-book)
Subjects: LCSH: Sunzi, active 6th century B.C.--Juvenile literature. | Generals--China--Biography--Juvenile literature. | Statesmen--China--Biography--Juvenile literature. | Military art and science--China--History--To 1500--Juvenile literature. | China--History, Military--To 221 B.C.--Juvenile literature. | China--History--To 221 B.C.--Juvenile literature.
Classification: LCC U55.S78 C66 2018 (print) | LCC U55.S78 (ebook) | DDC 355.0092 [B] --dc23
LC record available at https://lccn.loc.gov/2016058600

Editorial Director: David McNamara
Editor: Molly Fox
Copy Editor: Rebecca Rohan
Associate Art Director: Amy Greenan
Designer: Jessica Nevins
Production Coordinator: Karol Szymczuk
Photo Research: J8 Media

Printed in the United States of America

TABLE OF CONTENTS

INTRODUCTION

How many things do we encounter in our lives that are more than 2,400 years old? How many of us can say we have read and enjoyed a book about military strategy? How often do we look for a philosophy that can be applied to our lives to make them more worthwhile, and less confusing? Sun Tzu, by authoring *The Art of War*, can lead us to interesting answers to each of these questions.

Sun Tzu was probably just an ordinary person like you or me. He probably woke up each morning and ate breakfast, went to school, did his chores, and studied before falling asleep. What made him different was not birthright or extraordinary circumstances. What made Sun Tzu different was his ability to look at circumstances and formulate a plan for what to do next.

As each of us has a special talent or aptitude for learning a particular subject, so too did Sun Tzu. From an early age, it was clear that he had strengths in several areas of the military arts. He was able to apply critical thinking and careful planning to the problems of conflict and overcome his adversaries

The time in which Sun Tzu lived was not a peaceful time in history. This was especially true in the area of modern-day China where he lived. It was more than 2,400 years ago in the year 544 BCE, a time in which there were few other civilizations that still exist today. And even among those civilizations that existed during Sun Tzu's time, many did not have the technological

Opposite: Shang Dynasty swords on display in Binzhou City, China

advancements or careful recordkeeping that ancient China had. When learning the history of nearly any other country in the world, there would be no information dating back this far. Even among tribes that passed careful oral traditions from generation to generation, much of the time in ancient history has been forgotten or made into folklore. This is not the case in China, where historians kept records as early as Sun Tzu's time. Despite predictable inaccuracies between the two major texts from this time, we have historical data as far back as China's first emperor in 2698 BCE, because these records were carefully taken and then preserved for thousands of years.

Sun Tzu would eventually record his teachings about warfare and tactical combat in thirteen chapters, in a book called *Sunzi Bingfa* or *Sun Tzu's Art of War*. You may be wondering, how interesting can a book about military tactics be? Although the chapters do lay out many strategies for combat, the lessons within the book can easily be applied to other areas of life. His analogies often involve aspects of nature that are readily understandable and provide complete understanding of the subject matter. Additionally, though you are reading it in translation if you read the English version, in a good translation (such as the **Lionel Giles** version from 1910) the language flows beautifully and reads almost like a narrative instead of a series of rules for managing conflict.

Sun Tzu is a very important name, not just in Chinese history, but in the Western world as well. But some people doubt that he existed at all. Around the twelfth century CE, some scholars began to point to anachronisms between accounts of his life and questioned why he wasn't mentioned more often, if at all, in historical texts based on his importance in the era. Surely, a man who had so great an impact on the course of Chinese history, and even the history of mankind, would have been remembered by scholars of the period? Those who doubt his existence also point out the mention of cavalry and crossbows in *The Art of War,* which weren't developed until after Sun Tzu's supposed death. This causes some to question the authorship of the book.

Meanwhile, many scholars still believe that Sun Tzu was an important general in the Wu army, who claimed victory at one of the most pivotal battles of the Wu State, and legitimately authored the famed military text that he is credited with. As we lack decisive historical data, and archeologists have yet to uncover the many mysteries of China, we may never find out who is right.

A note for readers: China has historically used symbols in their written language. Instead of letters in an alphabet, each word has a specific symbol or set of symbols, and these symbols can change when used in combination with one another. As there is no accurate English translation for these symbols, the symbols are Romanized, or made into English words based on phonetics and semantics. There are two major ways to Romanize Chinese language for English readers. The first, Pinyin, is more straightforward in appearance and more commonly used in popular culture. The other, the Wade-Giles system, is more true to phonemes, but much harder to understand when written. Scholars have used this system in many books and papers about Chinese history. Since they are used in different ways, the author tried to include both versions for every Chinese language word to give a broader view of the language of China. The preference was given not to one system or the other, but rather whichever version was more popularly known. You will see examples of this frequently. One notable example is the **Battle of Baiju**, which can also be written the Battle of Boju. Every effort was made to keep both versions whenever possible.

CHAPTER ONE

The Culture *of* China in *the* Late Spring *and* Autumn Period

The **Spring and Autumn Period** is one of three time periods that make up the 800-year rule of the Zhou Dynasty. Sandwiched on either side by the **Western Zhou** Period and the Warring States Period, the Spring and Autumn Period is distinguished by political unrest and religious and philosophical exploration. The Spring and Autumn Period occurred between 771 BCE and 476 BCE.

Zhou Dynasty

The Zhou Dynasty (sometimes written Chou) was the longest in Chinese history, running from 1046 to 256 BCE. It followed the Shang Dynasty (1600-1046 BCE) and preceded the Qin Dynasty (221-207 BCE). The date of the beginning of the dynasty is noted as the **Battle of Muye**, when King Wu defeated the Shang,

Opposite: Sun Tzu is frequently represented throughout Chinese art and history.

A map of China during the Spring and Autumn Period would look much different than a map of contemporary China.

ending their reign. It is said that the Shang Dynasty was so corrupt in the end, that slaves who were forced to fight for them against the Zhou turned their spears upside-down as a sign that they didn't support the Shang. Many defected and fought instead on the side of the Zhou. Not only did they lose many soldiers

this way, but it also affected the morale of the army. King Wu, advised by strategist Jiang Ziya, easily won the battle and took control of the country. He and his followers justified the change in rulership under the **Mandate of Heaven**, a thought process which said that there could only be one true ruler in China at a time. According to the mandate, whoever fought most valiantly and won power was chosen by the gods to rule, and did so with their blessing.

Despite corruption at the end of the Shang Dynasty, most of their reign had been one of peace and tranquility in China. The stability under Shang rule had allowed many developments in Chinese culture, such as the development of recordkeeping, bronze working, and jade carving to develop. The Shang kings were known for ruling *for* the people instead of at their expense or just for the enjoyment of power. They developed irrigation systems and grew more practical crops, like millet and wheat, and domesticated animals like dogs and even silkworms. The last king of the Shang, Shang Chou, was a cruel man. He turned away from the good example set by previous kings and became most well-known for his torture tactics. He ruled with fear, and in doing so, created widespread disillusionment within his kingdom. This allowed the Zhou to take control.

The Zhou Dynasty built upon the foundations of the Shang developments, continuing irrigation projects to provide water for crops to further districts in China that had previously gone without. The introduction of ox-drawn plow carts and new ideas about crop rotation increased crop yields, ensuring health and prosperity for most. The introduction of horseback riding and infrastructure advances, like roads and canals, increased mobility and communication throughout the country. The first coin systems, paired with these advancements, made large-scale trade viable for the first time.

Several other important advancements in Chinese history occurred during the Zhou Dynasty, including the invention of cast iron, which could be used to create incredibly strong tools and weaponry that were more versatile than previous incarnations. They also continued to use bronze casting to create tools, vessels, and objects of great beauty. Gravesites from this time often contain bronze and jade trinkets, giving us insight into craft-making of the era.

Western Zhou Period

The Western Zhou Period, which began the Zhou dynasty, went from 1046–771 BCE. It is considered to be a golden age in Chinese history. The leaders of this era, particularly under King Wu, King Cheng, and King Kang, were kind rulers and diligent in political affairs, making it a happy and peaceful time to live in China.

Bronze and jade trinkets representing animals have been found in gravesites dating to the Zhou dynasty.

Under the early Zhou kings, the country was restructured into a political system that closely mirrored **feudalism** in European countries. City-states existed throughout the region that controlled the surrounding farmland. The land was parceled out to noblemen, mostly lords and dukes, who in turn paid the king tribute for use of the land they controlled. In addition to paying tribute, they also pledged to follow the king's commands and send knights into the king's armies if requested. In return, the king allowed these nobles to profit from the land they controlled and make most decisions regarding their states. Rulers of each state were given ownership not just of the land, but of the people in their state. This system was called the **Fengjian (Fenfang) system**.

At the end of the Western Zhou Period, 148 small states, mostly consisting of a single city and surrounding farmland, were recorded. Each of these had a distinct lord or ruler, who essentially acted as king of his own small kingdom. If problems arose, particularly dissent or rebellion in the smaller states, the army would be sent to remove that leader and replace him with another ruler who was loyal to the king. The lords of these city-states were given so much power that each state had their own currency and tax system that were not regulated by the king or his government. Though the rulers of each state paid tribute to the king, they rarely interacted with him in any other way.

While the Fengjian system is similar to feudalism, the most notable difference is kinship among the ranking officials and noblemen. Unlike the European system, in which noblemen would often be chosen for their talent, under the Fengjian system the king would send family members, either those in his blood line or those acquired through arranged marriages, to rule regionally and locally. This allowed people in subservient positions to serve the head of the family as opposed to a ruler-king, making the system very successful in the early years of the dynasty. King Wu, for instance, had forty family members serve as vassals, and fifteen of those were his brothers. His family members accounted for more than half of his seventy-one total vassals.

During this time, people were broken into castes called "**The Four Occupations**," or "The Four Categories of People." While these occupations determined much about a person's future, people were not born into these classes. They could choose to change their profession, for example, and thus change their classification. These four classes, in order of respectability, were the *shi (shih)*, or scholars; the *nóng*, peasant farmers; the *gōng*, who were craftsmen; and the *shāng*, who were merchants and tradesmen. The classes dressed differently, with the major difference being that the *shi* wore flowing robes while the other three classes wore pants or trousers to facilitate their work. These distinctions were not thought to be about social standing in the beginning and weren't considered to be of great importance until the Warring States Period, when a distinct stratification occurred. During this time, the *shi* would emerge as great military leaders and philosophers. Later dynasties would use these classifications to suppress or manipulate ideas and to select government officials.

The fourth king, King Zhao, and the fifth king, King Mu, saw the beginning of social unrest in the kingdom. During this time, there were concerns about rebellion and difficulties controlling the people to the far east of the country, living in the Eastern Plain. Toward the end of the Western Zhou period, power was decentralized due to wars being fought on the borders, and the system began to break down. The king could no longer afford to appoint family members to each post, and instead had to choose people for their skill, which led to powerful leaders taking control of states and beginning to try to expand their borders. Chaos began to creep into the dynasty as they were attacked on all sides. In one instance, northerners, called **barbarians**, overran the capitol city of Haojing, killing King Xuan's young son, King You. This forced the royal family to abandon the city and flee to the East. This event is considered to be the beginning of the Eastern Zhou period, commonly called the Spring and Autumn Period, in 771 BCE. This time period also marks the beginnings of the rise of Qin power, as they were tasked with holding off invasions in the North and steadily gained more military power. The Qin would eventually overthrow the Zhou to gain control of China using the same Mandate of Heaven logic that the Zhou had used to justify the change in rulership.

Spring and Autumn Period

In 771, the Spring and Autumn Period began. While it is sometimes called "Eastern Zhou," to denote the capitol city being moved to Luoyi (Chengzhou), it is most commonly called the Spring and Autumn Period for the *Spring and Autumn Annals (the Chunqiu Shidai)*, written by Confucius during this time.

During this period, the Zhou dynasty began to decline, though the change was slow at first. The individual lords of the states started to become more and more powerful, causing military unrest. The smaller states began to fight amongst themselves, trying to usurp power from one another. As the individual states grew more powerful, they began to ignore the already vague central government of the king and increase their own interests by overtaking smaller states. These conflicts eventually grew so strong that during the Warring States Period, the Zhou dynasty lost all control over their outlying states, and smaller kingdoms, called **hegemons**, would emerge.

The Spring and Autumn Period was also a time of unparalleled philosophical advancement in Chinese history. It was during this time that both Confucius and Lao-Tzu are thought to have lived, founding two of China's major religions: Confucianism and Taoism (also written Daoism). This time in history is sometimes referred to as the "**One Hundred Schools of Thought**." During this time, schools of philosophy flourished, and because of the open exchange of philosophical and religious ideas, many new concepts developed around the country. Since the small fiefdoms often had their own languages and traditions, it was possible for many different schools of thought to coexist without angst. Due to advancements in infrastructure, the exchange of ideas from one part of the kingdom to another was facilitated, and people began to exchange intelligent ideas about philosophy and religion across borders. Schools flourished and education excelled, creating a renaissance of sorts to occur throughout China.

In later years, the first Emperor of Qin would require all religious and scientific texts that he did not personally agree with to be destroyed, so many of the ideas from that time period are lost. Despite repeated book burnings, Confucianism and Taoism have persevered into modern times, regardless of his insistence that they were corrupting the people in his kingdom and were fundamentally wrong.

Confucianism

Confucianism is one of the oldest structured philosophies that is native to China. While it is sometimes called a religion today, its teachings were originally imparted as secular wisdom. The moral code that Confucius created for society is much more about behavior for society's sake than about any divine or spiritual practice.

The beliefs of this practice are founded upon five basic virtues; *Ren* (charity), *Yi*, (righteousness) *Zhi* (knowledge), *Xin* (integrity), and *Li* (propriety). Followers of Confucianism believe that if all people followed these proscribed behaviors, it would create a perfect society. Confucius himself advocated that if each person were to accept their role in society and fulfill it, society could achieve harmony and people could live in a state of peace. Confucius is said to have developed the "Silver Rule," which is

Confucius is still considered one of the most important characters in Chinese history, though he lived more than 2,000 years ago.

like Western culture's "Golden Rule:" *Never impose on others what you would not choose for yourself.*

Confucius, the creator of Confucianism, was born around 551 BCE, in the state of Lu. The *Spring and Autumn Annals,* which he wrote, give the time period in which he was born its name. He was born Kong Qiu, but was later called Kong Zi (sometimes written Kongzi,) which means "Teacher Kong," or Kong Fuzi (meaning "Grand Master Kong" or "Great Teacher Kong"). He would not be known as Confucius until around the sixteenth century, when Christian missionaries began calling him by this name, most likely as a mispronunciation of Kong Fuzi.

He was born into the *shi* caste, which sat between aristocracy and the common man, though he was directly descended from kings of the Shang Dynasty. Despite being taught at a school for commoners, and living a fairly normal life through his early adulthood, Kong Qiu would go on to be one of the most important people in the history of China. He began to travel and seek out knowledge in his teens, becoming learned in the six arts of China, which were ritual, music, archery, charioteering, calligraphy, and mathematics. He also learned classical poetry and studied history, which made him a desirable mentor by the time he reached his thirties. Despite his mastery, he believed that all children should receive an education and refused to limit his classes to children of noblemen. In his later years, he would go on to serve in governmental positions, such as magistrate, where he hoped to influence policy to reflect a moral code for the good of society.

Many of his discussions with his students and with government officials, often containing parables to illustrate the reason behind his teaching, are recorded in the **Four Books**

and Five Classics of the Confucian Canon. His teachings are still admired throughout the world and studied for their moral implications and beauty.

Taoism

Another philosophy that arose during the Spring and Autumn Period is Taoism, which emphasizes living in harmony with oneself and others. Tao or Dao, which means "way," is the life-force in all beings and things, according to Taoists. It is both greater than all of these things, and within all of these things. It underlies everything in the universe and can be thought of as everything and nothing. While originally Taoism did not include any gods or goddesses, some modern variations worship historical figures of great importance, like Confucius and Taoism's founder, Lao Tzu (Lao Zi). Some even worship natural forces like the moon, the sun, and the tides. Despite these variances, Taoism is not a religion in the strict sense of the word, but rather a way of achieving balance in life.

The ultimate goal of Taoists is to live selflessly. They are encouraged to listen to their elders and treat their parents with the utmost respect, to love one another and perform acts of kindness, to abstain from alcohol and exercise daily, and to follow a set of rules created for the good of society, which mirror many of the Western philosophies: do not kill, lie, steal, cheat, or judge others.

It is unclear if Lao Tzu, credited as the founder of Taoism, was a real person. Due to the lack of biographical information about him, some scholars of the period believe him to be the embodiment of a school of thought, a conceptual person used to illustrate a teaching, rather than a historical figure. Despite this, the earliest texts attributed to Lao Tzu date back to the sixth century BCE, which is the Spring and Autumn Period of the

Lao Tzu's writings in the *Tao Te Ching* are still widely read and continue to inspire people to live in harmony.

THE FOUR BOOKS AND FIVE CLASSICS

During the Spring and Autumn Period, some of the most important historical texts in Chinese history were written. While historians debate the authorship of these four books and five classics, the nine books that make up the "The Confucian Canon," they all agree that Kong Qiu, or Confucius, had a hand in them. It is widely believed that if Confucius was not the author of these texts, that he was at least the editor who "fixed up" the originals in his old age, or at the very least, the man who compiled the contents.

The four books consist of *The Great Learning, The Doctrine of the Mean, Analects, and Mencius*. The five classics consist of *Classic of Poetry, Book of Documents, Book of Rites, I Ching,* and *Spring and Autumn Annals*.

The four books are mostly collections of the teachings of Confucius. They are categorized by theme and include wisdom on how to behave in society and personal growth through virtue and the pursuit of knowledge. The second two, *Analects* and *Mencius*, convey his teachings through recorded conversation. In *Analects*, the speeches of Confucius and his discussions with disciples are recorded, while in *Mencius*, the scholar Mencius is recorded in his dialogues with kings, which contains much more effusive language than the other texts.

The five classics serve a different purpose. The *Classic of Poetry* is a collection of poems, songs and hymns collected by Confucius from among the most important of his time. *The Book of Documents,* the oldest text in the collection, dating back to sixth century BCE and the *Spring and Autumn Annals* are records of the time, including narratives on birth, death, and significant events during the Zhou Dynasty. The former also includes the earliest examples of Chinese prose.

The Book of Rites describes the rituals practiced during the earliest periods in China, including sacrifices and court ceremonies. The *I Ching* or *Book of Changes* is an explanation of the earliest divination in China.

These texts served as the original curriculum in China and were used as the basis for all civil examinations during the Ming and Qin Dynasties. They are still studied in modern China and considered to be the basis of both Confucian thought and modern Chinese philosophy.

Zhou dynasty. The common mythology associated with Lao Tzu indicates that he was born as a wise old man, complete with white hair, straight from the womb. They claim that he left his job as head librarian of the Imperial Archives one day and rode off on a giant ox to escape the disappointment of humanity. On his way, he was stopped and prevented from going any further unless he wrote down his teachings for all of mankind. Due to this, he is often pictured on an ox. This text, called the *Tao Te Ching*, or *Doodejing*, is still widely read today, and proscribes a daily practice to bring about harmony in oneself and with all things. The practice of Tai Chi would evolve from his teachings around 440 CE.

The Art of War, Sun Tzu's military treatise written at around the same time, is heavily influenced by Taoism. Most of the practices put forth in *The Art of War* come directly from Taoist beliefs and use ideas of harmony and balance to succeed in battle.

Warring States Period

In 476 BCE, when the central government had lost all control and the smaller governments were struggling with one another for power, the Zhou dynasty reached its last leg. As individual states fought for power, the Zhou's authority simply faded away. Having less authority than ever, the Zhou dynasty began to recede in importance as other states merged, eventually forming eight warring states that feuded with one another. Despite repeated attempts to conquer one another by all eight of these kingdoms, the Qin would eventually be victorious, claiming the Mandate of Heaven and taking control in 221 BCE. Qin Shi Huang would be crowned the first emperor of China that year.

Daily Life

People of this era began to adopt new religious ideals and seek philosophical education, relying more on science and less on superstition than their ancestors had. This did not mean that they had completely forgotten many former practices, which did not immediately fade away. For instance, many people today still pay respect to their dead ancestors, a practice that was common during the Zhou Dynasty. It was believed that the spirits of ancestors guided a person's destiny, and disrespect to them could lead to a change in fortunes.

Fortune telling was commonly practiced during the Zhou Dynasty, as it had been during the Shang Dynasty. The most common way this was done was with **oracle bones.** Oracle bones were used to ask questions of the ancestors, in order to gain insight into troubling situations and seek the wisdom of those gone before. This was done by taking the bones of a slaughtered animal, usually a breastbone or shoulder blade, and writing a question on the bone before using a hot metal rod to crack the bone in half or puncture it. Often, two possible outcomes would be listed, and the way in which the bone cracked would give the answer. Sages interpreted the cracks to gain insight into situations.

Traditional folklore indicated that the king controlled the weather. It was the king's job to please the sun gods and the rain gods to ensure a good harvest. By making sacrifices, both animal and human, the king would ensure the harvest was plentiful, and thereby would take care of his subjects. During the Zhou Dynasty, this tradition shifted from the use of living creatures, both animal and human, to the use of clay effigies as sacrifices.

While royalty could afford to eat meat or fruit, common Chinese people did not eat these things unless it was a very special occasion. They mostly ate rice in the south, or wheat and millet,

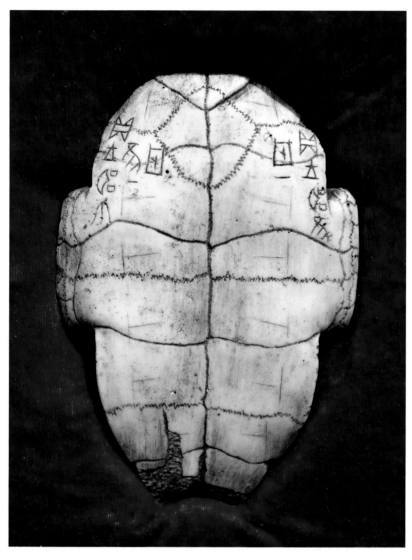

Oracle bones were used as a form of divination in ancient China.

which was boiled like rice, in the north. They would sometimes put soybeans, introduced as a crop during the Zhou Dynasty, on their rice for extra fat. As irrigation expanded, people began to grow their own vegetables (cucumber and bok choy were common) to eat with rice. Chopsticks were allegedly invented around this time and would quickly become the most common eating utensils in China.

During the Spring and Autumn Period, trade expanded, and new foods made their way into China, including sugar and sweet oranges. The Chinese also began to keep bees in apiaries for honey and wax. This was the beginning of the **Silk Road**, which would persist for thousands of years. Traders used horses and camels to transport spices from India, ivory and gold from Africa, and perfume and figs from Europe, to trade for silk and pottery in China. Tea, which would become the traditional drink of China, was introduced during the Zhou dynasty and was popularly traded on the Silk Road. Despite this, it was still much more common for people to drink fermented beverages, similar to modern-day beer, than tea during this time period.

Military Importance

As the Zhou Dynasty began to fail, military strategy began to become more important for all of the states of China. As states began to usurp power from one another and became increasingly powerful, they began to seek out skilled warriors to help them fight rival nations and to gain control of more land. They spent time and money to train their armies and build up their numbers in anticipation of war. This is when the *shi* caste began to shift into the role of military strategists. Many men became soldiers, military leaders, and expert advisors during this time, as these roles became associated with increased wealth and power.

As people began to study warfare, many advancements were made. The way in which battles were waged began to shift from attacks built on sheer numbers of warriors to psychological warfare. As people began to recognize the value of fighting smarter instead of fighting harder, the role of generals changed in battle.

There were also advancements made in weaponry during this time. Iron weapons allowed strong swords to be forged, and a shift from **chariots** leading troops into battle to cavalry and infantry made wars completely different than they had been at the beginning of the Zhou Dynasty.

Amid political unrest, scrupulous leaders searched out brave, talented generals and innovative methods of training their soldiers to go into battle. It was out of this developing school of military thought that Sun Tzu emerged, and during which time his classic book of warfare, *The Art of War*, became popular.

CHAPTER TWO

The Life *of* Sun Wu

I t was during the late Spring and Autumn Period that one of the world's greatest military leaders would emerge from the Wu state. While Sun Tzu (pronounced SOON-zuh) is credited with writing one of the most popular texts about warfare in the history of the world, there is little biographical information available about him. Most of what we do know has been gleaned from limited historical records of the time, or implied by historians who are scholars of ancient China, based on their knowledge of the culture and lifestyle of the time.

While many historians agree that Sun Wu, later called Sun Tzu, was an important general in the Wu army under **King Helu**, little else is known about his life. Many scholars of the era question if he existed at all, or if the name "Sun Tzu" is simply the personification of a school of military thought. Some have suggested that Sun Wu, the author of the most widely regarded military treatise in the history of mankind, was the name of a student of a great

Opposite: Sun Tzu was probably born with the name Sun Wu in or around the year 544 BCE.

A drawing of Sun Tzu as he may have looked in adulthood

military leader who recorded the teachings of his mentor. Other historians have implied that the work is a collection of the teachings of several military leaders, and that "Sun Tzu," which can be glossed as "Master Power," was used to remain anonymous while providing a credible author for the text. However, many other historians have since come to the conclusion that he was an actual historical figure, and credit him with sole authorship of *The Art of War*.

The Early Life of Sun Wu

Even among historians who believe in the **historicity** of Sun Tzu, the date of his birth is widely disputed. While some scholars place his birth as late as the year 536 BCE, the general consensus seems to be 544 BCE. There were, of course, no birth certificates at that time, and no surviving documents seem to give a detailed account of his birth. Most estimates of his birth date are extrapolations from records of his military career and the date of completion of his military treatise.

In fact, historians are not just divided about *when* Sun Tzu was born, but they also cannot agree upon *where* he born. The *Spring and Autumn Annals*, which is the official chronicle of the Chinese State of Lu from 722 to 481 BCE, lists his birthplace

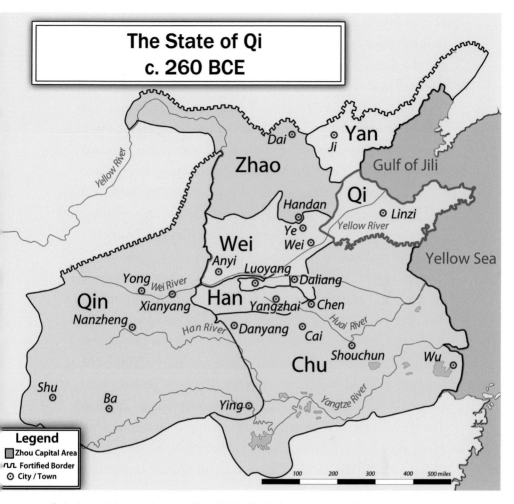

The State of Qi
c. 260 BCE

Yellow River

Dai
Ji
Yan
Zhao
Gulf of Jili
Handan
Qi
Linzi
Ye
Yellow River
Wei
Wei
Anyi
Luoyang
Daliang
Yellow Sea
Yong
Wei River
Han
Yangzhai
Chen
Qin
Xianyang
Danyang
Cai
Huai River
Nanzheng
Han River
Shouchun
Wu
Chu
Shu
Ba
Ying
Yangtze River

Legend
Zhou Capital Area
Fortified Border
City / Town

100   200   300   400   500 miles

Scholars debate whether Sun Wu's birthplace was Wu (lower right of map) or Qi (highlighted yellow area).

as Qi (sometimes written Ch'i), a peninsula in the Northeastern part of China that juts into the Yellow Sea, part of modern-day Shandong Province. However, *The Records of the Grand Historian*, known as the *Shiji* or "Scribe's Records," which covers the period in Chinese history from the **Yellow Emperor** to Emperor Wu of Han (about 2,500 years) differs on this point. This text lists his birthplace as Wu (also called Gonwu or Gongwu), which is still the name used to describe the region found in southeastern China. These two records are the earliest in Chinese history, but both have questionable authenticity since they may have been written or collected well after much of the recorded history took place. This means that there is a possibility of pieces of history being forgotten, exaggerated, or conflated with other times.

In addition to discussions over his authenticity, birth name and birthplace, even his name causes confusion among historians. Tzu (also written as *Zi,* meaning that Sun Tzu can also be expressed as *Sunzi* or *Sunwuzi*) is an honorific title meaning "master," which would have been given as a show of respect for his profound mastery as a teacher or philosopher. This means that Sun Tzu, "Master Sun," would not have been born with that name, but rather would have been given this title later in life, or possibly even after death. There are many examples of this honorific title in Chinese history. The great philosopher Confucius was called Kong Zi, "Philosopher Kong," and Lao Tzu (Laozi), the first Taoist, literally translates to "old teacher." Many people throughout Chinese history have become known as Tzu or Zi to denote their learned status and achievement in scholarly affairs.

Sun Tzu was most likely born with the name Sun Wu. His surname, Sun, would be listed first, as is the Chinese tradition. His given name, "Wu," while identical to the name of the state of Wu in English, would have been represented by a different character in Chinese. This is not indicative of where he was born. "Wu" may even have been a nickname, because it sometimes means "military," which would have been a fitting name for one so skilled in military reasoning. While we may never know exactly how he came to be called "Wu," in *The Records of the Grand Historian,* his biography bears the title, "Biography of Sun from Wu." The opening line translates to "Sunzi, whose name was Wu, was from the state of Qi."

He is sometimes recorded by the name "Quig Chun" in his teen years, meaning "still young." In the *Spring and Summer Annals,* this name is used for the person they believe to be Sun Tzu circa 516, which would make him roughly eighteen years old if he was born in 536 BCE, and twenty-six if he was born in 544 BCE. This is probably descriptive of his age, rather than the name he went by in his day-to-day life. His "**courtesy name**," which is a name by which a person was known outside of their family for formal or professional purposes, was Changqing or Chang Qing.

While the exact year of his birth is not known, there is one aspect of Sun Tzu's life that most historians agree on, and that is the fact that he was born in the late Spring and Autumn Period of China, which is generally listed as having occurred between 722 and 481 BCE. His actual birthday might not be known, but records of *The Art of War* appear as early as 510 BCE. This means he would have come of age either right before, or during, the Warring States Period in Chinese history, between 475 and 221 BCE. This would have made his military prowess particularly useful.

The Sun Family

Though we know little about Sun Tzu's family history, we do know that he was literate. This means that his family was most likely a part of the Chinese aristocracy, or the *shi,* the non-landowning aristocracy, since the *shi* were frequently scholars and often well-educated. While many *shi* were traveling academics, it was not unheard of for a *shi* caste member to work as a mercenary, as Sun Tzu seems to have done. He must also have been trained in military arts and Taoist philosophy in his youth, in order to have compiled his masterpiece, *The Art of War*, by the time he was appointed to King Helu's service. Little else is known about his childhood or teen years.

One possible family history that has been posited by historian Sima Qian explains Sun Wu's exemplary knowledge of the military arts and may even account for discrepancies in his birth place. He believed that Sun Wu was born into a well-respected military family, one who spent several generations in the service of the aristocracy in Qi. Based on limited records from the era, some historians have speculated that Sun Wu was directly descended from King Li of Chen, but that King Li's son, Chen Wan, fled to the state of Qi after being exiled during a period of bitter fighting within the royal family. When Chen Wan arrived in Qi, he changed his surname to Tian, and so became Tian Wan. He served King Huan, then ruler of Qi, as a **gongzheng**. A gongzheng is a high-ranking official in charge of handicraft. Throughout the next several generations, the family would continue to serve the royal family of Qi under the name Tian, until Sun Wu's grandfather, Tian Shu, made himself notable as a mercenary warrior.

Tian Shu had a small fiefdom in Le'an and was a well-respected man. In his service to the king, he went into battle several times, proving himself to be a wise military strategist and valiant warrior. For these feats, the king gave him a new surname; Sun, which roughly translates to "power." And thus, the Sun family was born. The Sun family would pass on their military expertise from generation to generation, directly influencing the military affairs of China for hundreds of years.

It is unclear whether Sun Wu was born in Qi or Wu; however, it is probable that his father, Sun Ping, moved the family from Qi to Wu during Qi's civil war. Whether this move took place prior to or after Sun Wu's birth is unknown. Sun Wu most likely studied military arts from his grandfather, who was known for his superior tactical skill. He would go on to use the training handed down from his family in conjunction with Taoist beliefs to recreate the way people thought about war.

Military Success

While living in Wu, Sun Wu befriended a man named Wu Yun, though he was better known by his courtesy name **Wu Zixu**, who had defected from the state of Chu after his father and brother were put to death by the King of Chu. He was impressed with Sun Wu, and after many conversations about military arts, Wu Zixu, who was the principal advisor to King Helu of Wu, recommended his friend to the king.

By this time, Sun Wu was already considered a master of the military arts. He had collected his teachings on battle into a book which is referred to as *The Thirteen Chapters* (later becoming *The Art of War*) which contained thirteen chapters of strategy and thoughts about military leadership, all of which were heavily influenced by Taoist philosophy. At the urging of Wu Zixu, he presented this book to King Helu, who was very impressed by the work.

Sun Wu is Put to the Test

The famous story of this first meeting between Sun Wu and King Helu was recorded by Sima Qian in his *Records of the Grand Historian*. This story is said to illustrate both Sun Tzu's superior military abilities and his commitment to the principles laid out in his book.

After reading the treatise, King Helu asked if the principles in *The Thirteen Chapters* could be put to a test, to which Sun Wu agreed. "Even women?" the king asked, and Sun Wu answered in the affirmative, saying that anyone at all could be made a soldier with proper training.

To test his theories, King Helu gathered one hundred and eighty women together in front of his castle. The group included his many **concubines**. The king and his advisors then went to a pavilion overlooking the field to observe as Sun Wu began to train the women. Sun Wu broke them into two battalions, placing one of the king's favorite concubines at the head of each division as a commanding officer. He then went to the front of the assembled companies, and asked them if they knew the difference between right and left, and front and back. The women said they did. Sun Tzu then told them that he would give the instructions, and they would follow his words. If he told them to look forward, they would look straight ahead, and if he told them to turn left, they would turn toward their left hands, and so on. Once he was assured that they understood, he called for the drummer to begin, and to the beat of the drum he began to give orders. Instead of following the commands, however, the girls only laughed.

According to Sima Qian, Sun Tzu at this point said, "If words of command are not clear and distinct, if orders are not thoroughly understood, then the general is to blame." He checked for understanding once again, and being assured that women understood him, he called for the drummer to begin again.

He started the drills a second time, and once again the women were seized with fits of laughter instead of following orders. This time he said, "If words of command are not clear and distinct, if orders are not thoroughly understood, the general is to blame. But if his orders ARE clear, and the soldiers nevertheless disobey, then it is the fault of their officers." And so, he commanded that the two concubines appointed as the heads of each battalion beheaded.

The king, who had been watching from nearby, sent word to Sun Wu that he had passed the test, and that he needn't follow through with killing the women, hoping to dissuade him from killing his favorite concubines. Sun Wu replied that while acting in the capacity of general, he would not be able to honor the king's request to spare the women, and had them beheaded as the king and the other women looked on. He then appointed two new women to head each company, and once again began the drills. This time, the women complied, performing with perfect accuracy and in total silence. After several repetitions of the exercises, Sun Tzu sent word that the king could come and inspect his troops, saying, "They can be put to any use that their sovereign may desire; bid them go through fire and water, and they will not disobey."

This story was originally believed to be a parable, but upon studying *The Records of the Grand Historian,* many scholars believe in the historicity of this story in some form. While stories are often exaggerated in retelling, it seems likely that if Sun Wu was a real general, he also performed some test using the king's concubines to prove the points he laid forth in *The Art of War.*

After this, the king and his advisors saw that Sun Wu could handle an army, and he was appointed as a general. Some historians dispute this, claiming that professional soldiers (as opposed to appointing family members to position of military rank) were uncommon before the Warring States Period. However, if we are to believe that Sun Tzu was as gifted in the

The kings and emperors of China frequently had many concubines
who lived within the palace walls.

military arts as he seems to have been, he may have been an exception to this rule. During his time as a general, he would go on to conquer the capitol of the Chu state and would be so successful as a military leader that people from states far and wide would fear his name.

The Art of War

The most notable achievement in the life of Sun Wu is the authorship of the military classic, *The Art of War,* which is also known as *Sunzi Bingfa* or *Sun-Tzu Ping-fa.* This military treatise, which is compiled lessons about war and warfare, is still one of the most widely influential military resources in the world. Interestingly, the original title, *Sunzi Bingfa,* means "Sun Tzu's Military Principles." The title, *The Art of War,* does not come from any translation of the Chinese characters, but rather, from a distortion by early scholars.

While Sun Tzu had probably read texts on military theory when he was young, no books on warfare predating Sun Tzu exist. This makes *The Art of War* important both because of its content, but also because it is the earliest example we have of a military text in any part of the world.

Unlike several other popular studies on military tactics that are popular in the Western world, such as *Battle Studies* by the French colonel Ardant du Picq, or *On War* by the Prussian General Carl von Clausewitz, *The Art of War* has a distinctly East Asian feel. There is a spiritual element to the work that does not exist in Western tomes on war. Heavily influenced by the philosophy of the east and the military styles of ancient China, *The Art of War* is the oldest known collection of military tactics that is still used today. Despite having been written more than 2,500 years ago, it is still widely read and applied to subjects as wide ranging as battle and business.

In *The Records of the Grand Historian*, Sun Wu is described as having given King Helu a copy of the book upon their initial meeting, which would place the date of authorship shortly before 510 BCE. Some historians dispute that date, and, using references to military technology of the time and stylistic elements, date the completion of the book much later—sometime in the Warring States Period, which came after Sun Wu's death (if he was, as we assume, the author).

In the *Spring and Autumn Annals of Wu and Yue,* the author recounts this meeting:

> Sun Tzu, whose name was Wu, was a native of Wu. He excelled at military strategy but dwelled in secrecy far away from civilization, so ordinary people did not know of his ability. Wu Tzu-hsu [Wu Zixu, King Ho-Lu's advisor], himself enlightened, wise, and skilled in discrimination, knew Sun Tzu could penetrate and destroy the enemy. One morning when he was discussing military affairs he recommended Sun Tzu seven times. King Ho-Lu [Helu] said: "Since you have found an excuse to advance this shih [shi], I want to have him brought in." He questioned Sun Tzu about military strategy, and each time that he laid out a section of his book the king could not praise him enough.

Some historians had previously theorized that the book was completed around the middle of the Han Dynasty, or possibly even later, but recent archeological discoveries have allowed scholars to narrow the date much farther than before. In 1972,

Sima Qian (Ssu-ma Ch'ien) is one of Sun Tzu's most notable biographers.

SIMA QIAN

One of the most noted biographers of Sun Wu is Sima Qian, sometimes romanticized as Ssu-ma Ch'ien or Szuma Chien. He is most known for his *Records of the Grand Historian*, which is a series of biographies that covers 2,500 years of Chinese history. Though he lived during the Han Dynasty, and was probably born between 145–135 BCE, his history covers as far back as the Yellow Emperor, who died in 2598 BCE.

In his text, there is a chapter called "Biography of Sun from Wu," in which he mentions several parts of Sun Tzu's life, including a general completion date for *The Art of War* and the initial meeting between King Helu (Ho-Lu or Ho Lu are also used) and Sun Wu.

Sima Qian is also known for his biography of Sun Tzu's grandson, Sun Bin, who continued the family legacy of military leadership and published his own version of *The Art Of War*, called *Sun Bin's Art of War*, years after his grandfather had passed away. Sun Bin was also called "Sun Tzu," or "Master Sun," which confuses many historians, but Sima Qian seems to have distinguished between the two and determined their familial relationship in *The Records of the Grand Historian*.

construction workers accidentally uncovered a gravesite in the Yinque Hills outside of Linyi City in Shandong, exposing the *Yinqueshan Han Bamboo Slips.* The slips, ancient Chinese writing tablets made from strips of bamboo, included the text of two entire books. These slips included the previously lost *Sun Bin's Art of War,* which contained thirty chapters divided into two volumes (this was later amended by Cultural Relic Press to exclude the second volume after historians decided that **Sun Bin** had written only about half of the book) which had disappeared around the end of the Eastern Han Dynasty. The gravesite also contained the complete manuscript of *The Art of War,* containing all thirteen chapters in unusually good condition on a set of bamboo reeds. Some reeds were damaged beyond reconstruction, but of the reeds we can decipher, it seems likely that the book was being read almost as we know it today as early as the Western Han Dynasty. The bamboo slips containing these works have been dated between 140 and 118 BCE by archaeologists.

Some historians theorize that beyond the original text, modern volumes contain commentary and clarifications from military philosophers of later ages like Li Quan from the Jin Dynasty, nearly one thousand years afterward. As this volume was passed down from one generation to another, it is likely to have changed to some degree, but the discovery of the *Yinqueshan Han Bamboo Slips* had shown many historians how close modern volumes are to ancient volumes, despite later thoughts attributed to other authors that may have been included in later editions.

The Art of War didn't just change how people fought; it changed the way they thought about battle. While earlier military tales seem to imply that war was a gentlemanly sport in ancient China, Sun Wu takes it far more seriously. His methods for

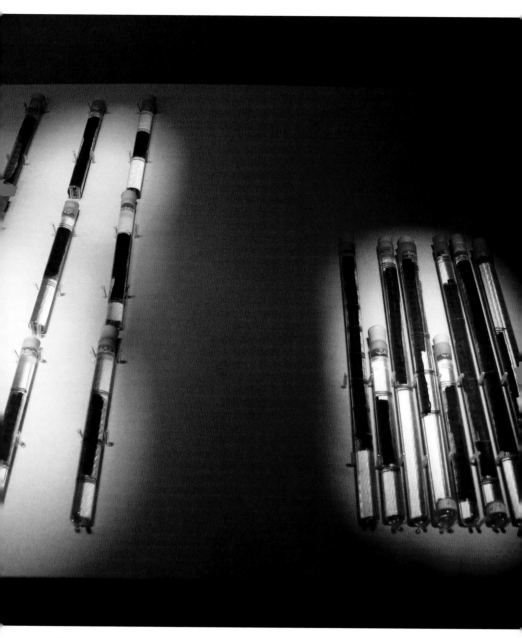

Bamboo slips recovered from the Yinque Hills contain the earliest existing copy of *The Art of War*.

managing conflict and winning battles imply abstinence from violence until it is of absolute necessity and encourage intelligence rather than brutality in all encounters. While many have used the treatise to gain power, the text itself is about exercising control rather than acting out of greed. In *The Illustrated Art of War*, published in 2005, translator Samuel Griffith writes, "In ancient China, war had been regarded as a knightly contest. As such, it had been governed by a code to which both sides generally adhered. Many illustrations of this are found … For example, in 632 BC the Chin commander, after defeating Ch'u at Ch'eng P'u, gave the vanquished enemy three days' supply of food. This courtesy was later reciprocated by a Ch'u army victorious at Pi. By the time *The Art of War* was written this code had been long abandoned."

Sun Bin's Art of War

Sun Bin (sometimes called Sun Pin) is thought to be a descendant of Sun Wu. Recorded history in China suggests that he was Sun Wu's grandson, fathered by Sun Wu's second son, Ming. Like his father, Ming was also a notable military strategist. Chronologically, this seems hard to believe, since even according to records of the era, he lived one hundred years after Sun Wu. Many more records of Sun Bin exist than of his alleged grandfather, Sun Tzu. In fact, for centuries historians thought that Sun Wu and Sun Bin may have been the same person because both were called "Sun Tzu," and both were exemplary military strategists.

Sun Bin studied under the well-respected recluse Guiguzi; he was considered brilliant by his teacher at an early age, partially because he had memorized *The Art of War.* One of his classmates, Pang Juan, whom Sun Bin considered a bosom friend, invited him to serve with him under King Hui of Wei. Sun Bin accepted. However, Pang Juan soon became jealous of Sun Bin's ability and framed him for treason. He was sentenced to death, though this sentence was reduced to face tattooing (to mark him as a criminal) and the removal of his kneecaps, and he left the state to seek refuge elsewhere. The name "Bin" can mean footless and probably refers to his disability.

While *The Art of War* recommends against siege warfare, Sun Bin's book details plans for succeeding in a siege. This is probably because Sun Bin was writing during the Warring States Period, during which time siege warfare became common as states attempted to overtake one another. This not only reinforces the date of completion for the original *The Art of War,* but makes Sun Bin's writing worthy of discussion without mentioning his grandfather's work. It appears that military prowess was familial, and that Sun Bin was a brilliant strategist in his own right, and not just as a descendant of Sun Wu.

The Later Life and Death of Sun Wu

Sun Wu is not mentioned again in any historical documents, so any information about his later life and death are wholly conjecture. Some believe that after taking Ying, Sun Wu wished to spend his remaining years in peace and retired from military service. There is no historical basis for this beyond what we know of his personality from historical documents and *The Art of War.* King Helu was injured during battle in 496 BCE and died from complications from that wound, probably on his finger. While

Many tributes to Sun Tzu exist throughout China, including this statue in Binzhou City.

武聖孫子

we know little more than that, the fact that we know of his death and Sun Wu is not mentioned probably means Sun Wu did not survive his patron. Due to this, historians who believe in the historicity of Sun Wu also date his death at 496 BCE. Due to Sun Wu's assertion that all war is deception, claims about his death may have been purposely made as a political tactic. The *Yueh Chueh Shu,* an early text about southern China by Kang Yuan, declares that "ten miles outside the city, there is a large tomb of the great strategist Sun Tzu." Unfortunately, unless new documents from the period are found, we will probably never know the truth of Sun Wu's death.

CHAPTER THREE

Waging War: *The* Military Conflicts *of* Sun Tzu

After King Helu recognized the great military abilities of Sun Tzu, he appointed him *Shanjianjun* (senior general) in his army. This was very unusual for the time, because professional soldiers did not begin to surface in China until the Warring States Period, which occurred after Sun Tzu's supposed death.

King Helu was an ambitious man and planned to extend the boundaries of his state into Chu territory. Not only did the two countries have a history riddled with trouble, but the boundary between the two states was often fought over from the time Wu was partitioned. Due to Sun Tzu's genius at commanding troops, and because of the sophisticated strategy laid out in *The Art of War,* the king tasked him with invading the state of Chu. Along with King Helu himself, his top advisor Wu Zixu, and his

Opposite: This mural depicts a battlefield in ancient China.

younger brother Fugai, Sun Tzu would lead the Wu military from a position of rank.

Although historians who favor the historicity of Sun Tzu usually assume that he was a great warrior, the Great Battle of Baiju (Boju) is the only battle in which Sun Tzu's presence is mentioned in any record that survives the time period. If Sun Tzu was, in fact, a general in King Helu's army, we can assume that he fought in many other battles as well. Unfortunately, we will never know the extent of his military career because these battles were not, for one reason or another, recorded.

A Brief History of Ancient Chinese Warfare

China is the oldest continuous civilization in the world, dating back as far as 6000 BCE (and possibly beyond). Due to their long history of precise recordkeeping and culture of holding onto traditional beliefs and customs, we have clear information about the history of conflict throughout Chinese antiquity. As we would expect from any country that has so long a history, there have been many battles both within China and against foreign enemies that have shaped the contemporary country we know today.

Some scholars have accused Chinese historians of having a "pacifist bias" about the history of China, tending to assert that the Chinese are much more peaceful than their European counterparts. This is due, in part, to the widespread interest in Confucianism, Taoism, and Buddhism that has continued to influence Chinese thought throughout Chinese history. It may also be, at least in part, because of *The Art of War*. Since it was the most widely used text on military strategy in the history of the country, and because Sun Tzu encourages violence only as a defense or in the direst situation, siege warfare is often played down or entirely ignored in Chinese records. Since the history of Chinese warfare tends to be viewed through a lens of peace instead of a lens of war, battles and descriptions of warfare are often looked at as incidental, even in the very bloody Warring States Period. This may skew some of the information we have about battles and warfare from the time, as well.

The Xia Dynasty

The earliest warfare recorded in China took place between conscripted peasant farmers and nomadic peoples with simple spears, arrows, and other crude stone weaponry assembled by hand. Prior to the Xia Dynasty (2200-1600 BCE), clans from several ethnic groups, often with strong family affiliations, banded together for protection and to provide structure for their limited society. During these early days, conflict often happened at a very personal level instead of between nations or states as we would later see.

The Xia, the first ruling dynasty of China, is largely known only through folklore since written accounts would not begin until the Shang Dynasty. While we know little of the warfare that took place during the Xia Dynasty, we do know that at some point chariots were developed, possibly after seeing this technology through Aryan invaders from the Eurasian Steppes in 1700 BCE. Chariots became an important part of warfare from their introduction though the Qin and Han Dynasties.

The Shang used spoke-wheeled chariots to overthrow the Xia, circa 1600. In folklore, it is said that they amassed over

Chariots may have been used in China as early as the Xia Dynasty (2100-1600 BCE), but were undisputedly being used by 1200 BCE.

1,000 chariots to defeat the ruling dynasty; however, modern historians believe this number to be closer to 70. Even generous estimates by archaeologists don't exceed 300. The earliest history of China was passed through an oral tradition before being recorded by Sima Qian around 94 BCE, which means that many of these stories were probably exaggerated for posterity or entertainment.

Charioteering would become one of the arts practiced by the Chinese elite as early as the Shang Dynasty. It was one of the six arts taught to students to encourage well-rounded academic development. While the first chariot is attributed to Xi Zhong of the Xia Dynasty, archaeological evidence suggests that they actually came much later— possibly as late as 1200 BCE, discrediting earlier claims that they were used to overthrow the Xia. Chariots from this time were made to carry three people: a driver, to steer the horses; an archer equipped with bow and arrows; and a warrior equipped with a weapon or weapons of hand-to-hand combat.

The Shang Dynasty

During the Shang Dynasty, weapons improved vastly, partially because of the use of bronze casting. Prior to the production of bronze, most weapons were made from stone and were unwieldy. Bronze also allowed for weaponry like swords and arrowheads to have sharper, more deadly blades than stone weaponry.

A compound bow was developed during the Shang Dynasty, which could improve an archer's accuracy as well as the force behind each arrow. Crossbows would later become the hallmark of the Chinese army as simple bows underwent technological advances. Warriors of this time favored the **dagger-axe** (*gē*) in hand-to-hand combat, which was a long-handled weapon mounted with a dagger's blade and ax head on opposite sides of the end of the shaft.

Bronze or leather shields and helmets were sometimes used for protection, but armor at this time was reserved for nobility. Because nobles typically rode on chariots, weight was not a consideration in construction of early armor, nor was mobility. Typical armor of this time would be made from the boiled hide of an animal, usually a rhinoceros or a buffalo, that was then sometimes covered with a red lacquer to harden it. Early armor was constructed as a single piece on wooden dummies and did not take the size of a warrior into account, let alone his ability to move freely.

A typical army of this time would consist mainly of peasant farmers conscripted by noblemen. The king would personally lead

A dagger-axe blade dating to the Shang Dynasty

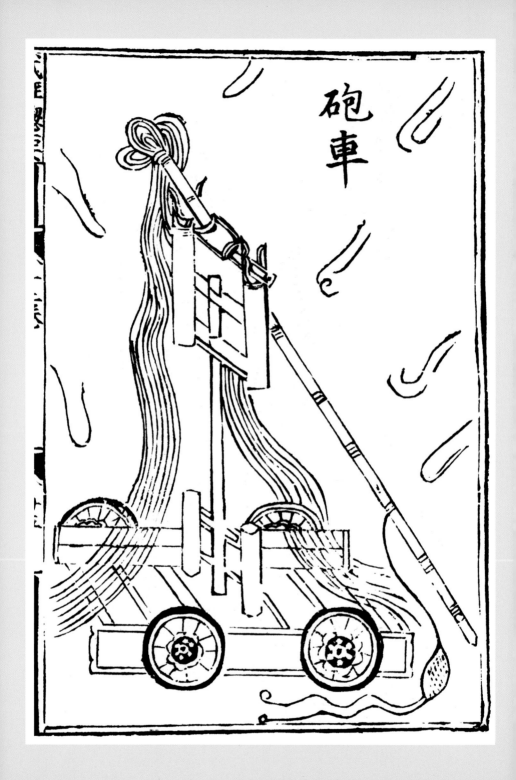

THE TREBUCHET

One military advancement to come out of China between the fifth and third centuries BCE is the trebuchet, a sling weapon that extends the power of the catapult and is the precursor to the cannon. While the trebuchet was a large weapon, it was well worth its weight when brought into battle.

A trebuchet includes a sling attached to a beam that is mounted on a spinning arm to fling heavy stones or other objects with more force. Trebuchets were commonly used in siege warfare, to break down walls or invade fortresses and castles. While the trebuchet was developed in China, it was used in much of medieval Europe as well, before the invention of gunpowder made the cannon a better option. In early accounts of Chinese warfare, dating to the Spring and Autumn and Warring States Periods, the trebuchet is mentioned as having flung not just heavy stones but sulfur bombs as well. The Chinese also reportedly added trebuchets to the tops of battleships in their navies.

The earliest trebuchets had troops of soldiers pulling on ropes at either end of the device, but later incarnations included a fixed counterweight that increased the velocity of the objects flung from its beam and reduced the amount of work it took to effectively use the machine. This made it easier to reload and reduced the amount of time between strikes, as well.

Opposite: The trebuchet was an important military advancement for Chinese warriors.

the army into battles, acting as commander and chief strategist. A typical army would consist of 5,000 peasants and a few elite warriors of noble background who acted as archers or charioteers. These people were not soldiers, per se, but farmers who were forced to fight when needed, and who returned to their regular jobs after the fighting was finished. In the case of insurrection, or when facing a foreign enemy with great numbers, the king might be able to amass as many as 13,000 troops to fight on his behalf, but these again were not skilled warriors trained in any military arts.

Western Zhou and Spring and Autumn Periods

Most of the technology associated with the Zhou Dynasty was simply improvements on existing technology left over from the Shang Dynasty. For instance, they still used the chariot, but Zhou chariots could be pulled by four horses instead of two, for increased speed. The chariots of this time also often had leather sides and sometimes an awning to protect those inside from enemy warfare and the elements.

In addition to better overall organization within military structures under the Zhou, there were three major military advancements in warfare during the first two periods of the Zhou Dynasty. The first was the use of iron to create weapons. While iron and bronze have only a slight difference in strength, iron had two major advantages: the first is that, once cast, iron is less likely to break apart than bronze. The second is that, unlike bronze, which requires both copper and tin to make, iron only needs iron. Needing one natural resource instead of two made creating weapons more efficient and much less expensive. Bronze continued to be the material of choice for weaponry throughout

Early armor in China was often constructed from bronze or leather.

this time but would eventually give way to iron when the demands of a larger army needed to be met.

The second important development in the Zhou period that lent itself to warfare was the creation of large ships resembling fortresses that could be used by a navy. There are no Western examples of this kind of ship, sometimes called a "floating castle." Prior to this time, Chinese warriors did not participate in naval affairs. A passage in Yuan Kang's *Yuejueshu* (*Lost Records of the State of Yue*) includes dialogue between King Helu and Wu Zixu detailing the kinds of ships they would bring to a battle, and while naval affairs were not very advanced in the Spring and Autumn Period, the beginnings of water warfare were definitely taking place.

The third, and arguably most important, military advancement during the Spring and Autumn Period was the use of the teachings in *The Art of War* to fight more strategic battles. Around the end of the Spring and Autumn Period, the text began to circulate among military leaders. By the end of the Warring States Period, many armies in China had adopted many of the techniques put forth in the text. The advice in the text suggested that strategic planning would win over brute force in every battle, so tactical changes began to take place within armies, and soldiers became much more organized by using ranking systems and military formations.

Under the Zhou, infrastructure also vastly improved, which made it easier to move large numbers of troops. Prior to this time, travel between states was difficult and often dangerous, but with better road systems, travel became much less tiring for horses and humans alike.

The Warring States Period

As the name suggests, this era was one of the bloodiest in Chinese history, riddled with wars for power within the country and against foreign enemies outside of the country. The **Seven Warring States** (though the number of states and their borders would fluctuate often during this period, often leading to some historians calling them the Eight Warring States) were Qin, Chu, Qi, Yan, Han, Wei, Yue and Zhao. These states would vie for power throughout the entire period until Qin eventually unified China as the new dynasty. Upon gaining control of all of the states in China, they shifted from the feudal system to a centralized power structure, allowing them to unite China for the first time in its history.

During this time, the size and style of armies changed considerably. Though chariots were still widely used at the beginning of this period, they began to lose favor as cavalry and infantry became more common. By this time, armies often exceeded 30,000 men, so chariots made less sense than creating formations of soldiers either on horseback or on foot.

The first Chinese cavalry can be traced to King Wuling of Zhao in 307 BCE. He thought that by imitating the dress of nomads, which meant wearing trousers instead of the robes that the military commonly wore in this period, and putting marksmen on horseback for better mobility (chariots were incapable of changing position quickly), that he would increase the efficacy of his armies. This was so effective that cavalries became common throughout the Warring States Period.

While the dagger-axe continued to be the most popular short range weapon, many had been adapted to include a spearhead for thrusting, and some had handles that were taller than the men that carried them. The Qin developed an eighteen-foot dagger-axe with a pike blade at the end that increased their efficacy during this period.

Armor was still too expensive and time-consuming to mass produce and was thereby still reserved for high-ranking soldiers and officials, but its structure changed considerably during this time. Instead of the single-piece constructions that were used in earlier periods, armor now consisted of a **cuirass**, which was a breastplate and backplate that fastened together on the sides under the arms. This left the arms and legs freer to provide better movement and make long-distance travel easier.

Armor of the Warring States Period was often made from leather or brass, and was either "coat of plates" or lamellar. The coat of plates is exactly what you would expect, where hundreds of small plates made from either leather or brass, which did not overlap, were stitched or riveted together to create a protective covering. Lamellar constructions had the plates overlapping, one on top of another, instead of lying flat like the coat of plates models, which allowed for more flexibility. As time went on, armor would become more and more intricate. This is particularly true for cavalries, who initially wore almost no armor at all to allow them to move freely, but by the end of the Warring States Period often wore full body armor, as did their horses.

Most of what we know about armor of the late Warring States Period and early Qin Dynasty comes from the archeological study of the famed terracotta warriors of the **Terracotta Army**. These effigies, discovered in 1974 in the Shaanxi Province by farmers trying to do nothing more than dig a well, are the largest collection of pottery figurines ever discovered in China. They were discovered just east of the Qin Emperor's Tomb and are believed to be a part of a much larger underground necropolis— one that may be as large as thirty-eight square miles!

The Terracotta Army gives an in-depth look at the stratification of the army that historical texts could not have conveyed so clearly. Some soldiers in the collection bear no armor and are smaller than the rest, causing archeologists to assume that they are conscripted peasants. The terracotta figures increase in size as their rank increases, though they are all roughly life-sized. Their armor, style of dress, and weaponry changes, too, as their rank changes. In addition to foot soldiers, cavalrymen complete with life-sized horses and chariots with their charioteers are included in the crypt. Despite the paint having faded and chipped away to almost nothing, we can see that these effigies were once quite lifelike and were probably intended to protect the emperor in the afterlife. The soldiers also once held real weapons, through most of them have been lost due to decay and looting. The weapons that do remain include spears, arrowheads, dagger-axes and crossbows, a popular weapon of the Warring States Period.

At the end of the Warring States Period, the Qin began to change the way their army was staffed. Instead of nobles leading the army, they began to hire talented generals. Instead of forcing peasants to fight in the army, they began to pay professional soldiers who were much more reliable and well-trained than their predecessors. This allowed the armies to fight well-executed campaigns with greater accuracy than ever before.

The Wu-Chu Wars

From 512–506 BCE, in the late Spring and Autumn Period, the states of Wu and Chu engaged in what would come to be

The Terracotta Army was discovered by accident when farmers in the Shaanxi Province were trying to dig a well.

known as the **Wu-Chu Wars**. During this time, the Wu Kingdom would reach the pinnacle of its power, before being eventually defeated and annexed by the Yue Dynasty during the Warring States Period.

Though the Wu-Chu Wars happened prior to the official beginning of the Warring States Period, they took place at the end of the Spring and Autumn Period, when the Zhou Dynasty was already failing and many states were warring to gain control of new land and power over their neighbors. What happened between Wu and Chu during this time was a precursor to what would happen in the entire country on a larger scale during the next several centuries.

Background

Wu began as a minor state within the state of Chu and remained this way for most of the Spring and Autumn Period. However, between 613 and 591 BCE, the state of Chu became a superpower and began to rapidly expand its borders. As Chu began challenging its neighbors' borders and threatening to overcome the central states, their rivals executed a plan to stop the Chu kingdom from overtaking other kingdoms nearby. This was called "allying with the State of Wu to check the State of Chu."

In order to keep Chu from expanding too far, the Jin, who were frequently warring with the Chu, forged an alliance with the Wu. They trained Wu armies in strategy, warfare, and charioteering, imparting all they knew about warfare to their new allies. As the Wu learned, they grew stronger and stronger. Soon, they had an army which surpassed the Chu in both skill and technology, if not in numbers.

In 584 BCE, with their new weapons and training, the Wu defeated the Chu for the first time. This marks the beginning of a period of seventy years during which they would be at war nearly constantly with one another. During this time, at least ten major wars would take place, and the Wu would consistently defeat the Chu, separating themselves into an independent kingdom with their own king.

Prior to this time, Wu was considered a barbarian state. Legend says that the state was founded by Taibo and Zhong Yong, the elder uncles of King Wen of Zhou. King Wen was also the father of King Wu, who was the first ruler of the Zhou dynasty, meaning that Taibo and Zhong Yong were nobility, regardless of whether they were considered a major state. Wu's inhabitants, who wore their hair short (the custom of the time was long hair) and were tattooed, were considered to be uncivilized by the other kingdoms in the dynasty. They did not participate in the politics or battles of China until after being trained by the Jin, late in the Spring and Autumn Period. Due to their status as a barbarian state, the Chu armies may have greatly underestimated them.

During the rule of King Ping of Chu, things took another dramatic turn. When King Ping married the bride of Prince Jian, previously named the successor of the throne, he also exiled Prince Jian to prevent any retribution later on. Prince Jian's top advisor, Wu She, and his eldest son, Wu Shang, were executed. His second son, Wu Zixu, barely escaped with the help of a physician living on the border of Chu, and took refuge in the state of Wu. Here, he became the most trusted advisor of Prince Guang, and vowed revenge against the King of Chu for his exile and his father's murder.

His chance came in 515 BCE, when he helped Prince Guang to execute his cousin, King Liao of Wu, and usurp the throne. Wu Zixu had long encouraged Prince Guang to claim the throne, as irregularities in passage of rulership had led to the crown passing to a new family instead of going to Guang, as it rightly should have. Under Wu Zixu's guidance, Prince Guang threw a banquet, during which he hired Zhuan Zhu, an assassin, to kill King Liao. Zhuan Zhu accomplished this by disguising himself as a chef and presenting a beautiful fish platter to the king. Despite being searched prior to going before the king, and despite the armed guards standing behind him, Zhuan Zhu killed the king with a knife hidden inside one of the fish on his platter. In folklore, this knife is called Yuchang, or "fish intestines," due to this method.

Prince Guang then ascended the throne, taking on the name King Helu (Ho Lu or Ho-Lu), and launched a massive campaign against the Chu kingdom.

The Great Battle of Baiju

In 506 BCE, King Helu and Wu Zixu, with the help of King Helu's younger brother Fugai, made plans to send forces into Chu. The king saw that the Chu were losing strength due to the wars they were fighting on several of their borders and realized that with their armies stretched thin, they would not be able to offer much resistance to yet another attack.

King Helu himself commanded the navy, which traveled westward on the Huai River, while Sun Tzu led an army on land. At the last moment, without explaining himself to the king, Sun Tzu changed his route, and his army landed on a cove of the Huai River. This route surprised the Chu forces, who were not able to correct their position quickly enough to stop Sun Tzu's army from penetrating deep into the Chu state through mountain passes along their border.

During the campaign, there was a point when Sun Tzu called for the troops to rest, bidding them to remain hidden until their strength had rallied. Though the king asked several times, Sun Tzu insisted that the proper time would reveal itself.

According to the *Zuo Zhuan*, an ancient book that was originally thought to be a commentary on the *Spring and Autumn Annals,* but is now considered an independent historical work, Fugai was one of the most prominent military figures present for this battle. He saw that the commanding officer for the Chu troops was a despicable man and that his troops did not respect him. He rightly predicted that his troops would not fight well, even though they outnumbered the Wu's forces, because they had a poor leader. When King Helu told his brother to wait before attacking, Fugai ignored him and led the first offensive with only 5,000 of his own men, achieving victory by employing lessons learned from *The Art of War.*

While King Helu's forces only numbered around 30,000 in total—and they were vastly outnumbered by the Chu warriors—by following Sun Tzu's advice, they were able to succeed. This allowed his troops to easily win in Baiju and then follow the retreating Chu forces to win five further battles. At one juncture, Fugai waited until half of the Chu army had crossed a river in retreat, influencing the numbers of enemy troops and easily achieving another victory. Yet another time, the Wu forces waited for the Chu army to take a meal and attacked them while they were eating. By waiting for their enemy to take a vulnerable position, to "reveal themselves" as Sun Tzu said, they had an advantage. They took the capital city of Ying, and King Zhou of Chu was forced to flee his home and take refuge in the southern part of the state.

Lasting Effect of the Battle of Baiju

Despite the military success that King Helu achieved during the Battle of Baiju, his success was short-lived. After the battle, Wu experienced the highest point in their kingdom in terms of power and authority, but it quickly came to an end.

One of the advisors of Chu, a man named Shen Baoxu, fled the capital city of Ying after Wu forces took over and went to the state of Qin to beg for assistance in defeating the Wu and reestablishing the Chu kingdom to its former glory. He was a former friend and contemporary of Wu Zixu from his days in Chu. According to folklore, Duke Ai of Qin initially refused to help, but Shen Baoxu persisted and cried in his courtyard for seven days. At the end of the week, moved by the man's commitment, he relented and aided the Chu warriors in defeating the Wu.

In 505 BCE, with the help of Duke Ai and his troops, the Wu were defeated in Ying, and the king of Chu restored to his capital. During the same time, Fugai attempted to usurp his brother's throne, and King Helu was called away from Ying to overthrow the coup. Fugai escaped to Chu, where he found refuge. The Chu state never returned to being the superpower it once was prior to the Wu invasion. The State of Wu would eventually fall to Yue troops in 473 BCE and become a part of that state.

Sun Tzu's Role in the Battle of Baiju

Just as historians cannot agree upon many facets of Sun Tzu's life, they also do not agree upon whether or not Sun Tzu was present at the Grand Battle of Baiju. Sima Qian mentions him at the battle in *The Records of the Grand Historian*, but the most accurate account of the battle, the *Zuo Zhuan,* or *Zuo's Commentary on the Spring and Autumn Annals,* does not mention him at all. While all historians agree that Wu rose to power using the strategies laid forth in *The Art of War,* some historians argue that if he were a real person, he must not have been present during this battle because he would have been a person of great importance to have been mentioned in the *Zuo Zhuan.* Other historians maintain his presence at the battle due to the work of Sima Qian, who has been found to be factually accurate at least as often as he was fanciful.

The Art of War in Battle

While Sun Tzu is only recorded in one battle throughout history, his work, *The Art of War,* has notably shaped many other battles in China and around the world. During the Warring States Period, many generals carried a copy with them as they went into battle. By the Qin and Han Dynasties, nearly every general had read the treatise and used Sun Tzu's methods in battle.

One notable battle fought and won with the aid of the information contained within *The Art of War* is the battle of Gaixia (called Kai-Hsia). This was the decisive battle on the Chu-Han Wars between 206–202 BCE. By this time, the Qin had conquered and unified China by ignoring the old rules of chivalry that had commonly prevailed in war. While this led to mass destruction of property and lives, both the Chu and Han had taken note of the effectivity of this strategy.

By using the strategy in *The Art of War,* the leader of the Han, Liu-Bang, was victorious. After this battle, he called himself the Emperor, and the Han Dynasty began.

KHI TAN

TATAR

HEICHEZI-SHIWEI

Huangdu

Z.Longhua

F.Fuyu

Xijing

Liaodong

Z.Ying

pyongyang

Songa

WHITE-TATAR

Z.Wu

YAN

Z.You

Z.Ping

Tiande

Z.Yun

BEI PING

Z.Sheng

Z.Shuo

Z.Ding

Z.Cang

Z.Deng

L.

SHUO FANG

JIN

Z.Zhen

ZHAO

Z.Qing

Z.Mi

Z.Xia

F.Taiyuan

Z.Yi

Z.Ling

DING NAN

Z.Xing

Z.Qi

Z.Hai

TANGUT

Z.Yan

QI

Z.Wei

Z.Jin

Z.Wei

Z.Yan

Z.Chu

Jiangdu

ang

Z.Hui

Z.Meng

Z.Xu

Z.Lan

Z.Wei

Xidu

Dongdu

Su

an

Z.Tong

Z.Zheng

Z.Ying

Z.Shou

F.Jinling

Z.Hu

Z.He

F.Fengxiang

L. LIANG

F.Xi

Z.Mi

Z.Qin

F.Tian'an

Z.Deng

Z.Guang

Z.Lu

Z.Xuan

Z.Wen

F.Xingyuan

Z.Fang

Z.An

WU

WU YUI

Z.Li

Z.Li

Z.Kui

Z.Gui

Z.E

Z.Jiang

Z.Qu

Z.Wen

Z.Mian

F. SHU

Z.Xia

F.Jiangling

Z.Wan

Z.Shi

Z.Hong

Z.Jian

Z.Han

F.Changle

F.Chengdu

Z.Yu

Z.Lang

MIN

Z.Rong

F.Changsha

Z.Jia

Z.Chen

Z.Qian

Z.Ting

Z.Quan

Z.Bo

Z.Yi

Z.Heng

Z.Zhang

KUNMING

CHU

Z.Yong

Z.Duyun

Z.Gui

Z.Ying

Z.Chao

Huichuan

ZANGKE

Z.Na

Z.Liu

Z.Wu

Z.Guang

umie

F.Shanchan

Z.Duan

CHANG HE

SOUTH HAN

Z.En

Z.Yong

Z.Lian

TOOTH

Z.Lei

Z.Feng

JING HAI

M.Le

Z.Jiao

BLACK TOOTH

Z.Ya

Z.Ai

CHAPTER FOUR

The Aftermath *of the* Battle *of* Baiju

T he aftermath of the Great Battle of Baiju, and the effect of using the techniques laid out in *The Art of War,* had both short- and long-term consequences that shaped modern China.

The Wu State

The Battle of Baiju is considered the first large-scale war of the Eastern Zhou, and as such, the precursor to the Warring States Period. Despite smaller battles leading up to this point, there had not been attack waged on so severe a scale before. Unrest was growing among the states in the Spring and Autumn Period, and because the Zhou Dynasty could no longer control the outlying states, there was nothing to prevent the rulers of the smaller states from succeeding and calling themselves kings.

Opposite: During the Warring States Period, borders of Chinese states were constantly in flux.

After capturing Ying, the capitol of Chu, King Helu considerably expanded his territory and influence. From 506 to 505 BCE, Wu was one of the strongest and most formidable states in all of China. However, because Wu's military was tied up in their battles with the Chu, the state of Yue, to the south, saw an opportunity to expand their boundaries by attacking Wu. Since King Helu's troops were diminished along the southern border, the Yue penetrated the Wu state, causing chaos. While Wu was able to hold off Yue forces initially, their troops were having trouble defending the state on two sides.

In addition to the Yue, the Qin had meanwhile been convinced by the official Shen Baoxu to aid the Chu. The Qin sent punitive forces into the city of Ying, the capitol of Chu, which had just been overtaken by the Wu. The Qin, who were known for their fierce warriors and extremely sharp swords, quickly overthrew Wu troops, causing them to retreat. By the end of 505 BCE, the Wu were engaged in battles on several borders, and these were long campaigns that left their forces exhausted and with limited supplies during the months of war.

Due to the precariousness of the situation, King Helu's younger brother, Prince Fugai, saw an opportunity to seize power from his brother. Fugai returned to Wu and declared himself the new king in his brother's absence. Perhaps he felt that his military success as the commander of troops at the Battle of Baiju entitled him to the throne, or perhaps he believed that his elder brother would die while engaged in battle on one of the borders, but most likely he believed that he and those loyal to him could effectively overtake King Helu's government. King Helu was forced to return to Wu to expel his brother, who sought refuge in Chu. While King Helu succeeded in removing his brother, the insurrection caused many in Wu to doubt him.

ZUO ZHUAN

While Sima Qian briefly records the Battle of Baiju in his *The Records of the Grand Historian*, the most accurate, detailed account of the battle can be found in the *Zuo Zhuan*, or *Commentary of Zuo*. It was originally thought to be authored by a blind disciple of Confucius, named Zuo Qiuming (hence the name), but there is little to no evidence to support this.

The *Zuo Zhuan* was originally thought to be exactly what it sounds like: a commentary on the earlier *Spring and Autumn Annals* work, which aims to clarify and create a narrative form for the *Annals*. However, most historians now believe it to be an independent work. Not only does the account expound upon many of the events in the *Annals*, but it also includes background information and insight into sayings and customs of ancient China. Its realistic yet elegant style and tendency toward third-person narration not only give us insight into the history of the time, but also establishes the ideal of classical Chinese writing, inspiring storytellers, poets, and authors to mimic the style of the work for centuries after it was written.

The account of the Battle of Baiju is a lively story that gives incredible detail about the Wu-Chu Wars, the battle itself, and the people involved in the dispute. One of the reasons that so many historians doubt the presence of Sun Tzu at this particular battle, despite being named as a prominent figure by Sima Qian, is that despite giving detail down to commentary on other parts of the battle, Sun Tzu is never once mentioned.

Warring in the Wu state continued throughout the rest of King Helu's rule. In 496 BCE, King Helu launched an attack on the state of Yue, who had previously opportunistically invaded them. The Yue quickly defeated the Wu and forced them back behind their own boundary, but King Helu sustained an injury. This injury would eventually cause complications that would kill the king. He died in 496 BCE. Some historians assume that Sun Tzu may have died in the same battle that killed King Helu, if not before.

Wu Zixu

While King Helu and Fugai are important historical figures, few men from this period are as glorified in modern culture as Wu Zixu. Following the Battle of Baiju, and the great success of King Helu's troops under Wu Zixu's leadership, Wu Zixu became a well-respected man. He was elevated to the status of Duke of Shen, and his name then became Shen Xu. This was a very prestigious honor reserved for heroes and those who were indispensable to the state.

Part of the folklore that surrounds Wu Zixu focuses on his desire to avenge his father's unjust execution at the hands of King Ping of Chu. Not only did Wu Zixu completely pledge his alliance to Wu after his father was killed, but he used many of the resources he had gained while living and working in Chu to defeat his former state. Upon entering the city of Ying, it is said that Wu Zixu opened King Ping's tomb and dragged his corpse into the street. He then administered 300 lashes with a whip to symbolically avenge his father's execution. While this may seem extreme to us in modern times, this gesture allowed Wu Zixu to receive justice for the wrongs against his family. For this, he is considered an example of filial piety.

While Wu Zixu was King Helu's most trusted advisor for his

Wu Zixu was a trusted advisor to the king of Wu, and a friend of Sun Wu.

entire rule, King Helu's son, Fuchai, did not share his father's confidence in the man. Fuchai was suspicious of Wu Zixu and consequently often ignored his advice. After King Helu's death in 496 BCE, when Fuchai ascended the throne, Wu Zixu's status was somewhat diminished, and he no longer served as the most valuable counsel to the king. The days of battle glory under Wu Zixu and Sun Tzu were quickly forgotten by the new administration, who lacked the shrewd nature of the previous king and his court.

In addition to growing mistrust of Wu Zixu, a new advisor was quickly gaining the new king's confidence. Bo Pi, whose grandfather was murdered by the government of Chu just as Wu Zixu's father had been, sought refuge in Wu and soon made the acquaintance of Wu Zixu. Wu Zixu recommended him to the king as an advisor, and soon the two were colleagues. However, it soon became clear that Bo Pi was not a respectable man. His questionable character would eventually be the downfall of Wu.

Wu Zixu feared that the state of Yue was a more formidable enemy than the Chu and advised King Fuchai to conquer the state of Yue before they grew too powerful. Bo Pi instead advised the king to continue to focus on defeating the Chu, who were a bigger and more powerful state. The king, already distrustful of Wu Zixu, decided to take Bo Pi's advice. Wu Zixu persisted in his warnings to the king that the Yue would soon be able to rise up against them from the south, until the king decided to punish Wu Zixu for sabotage.

Wu Zixu was given a sword and told to kill himself for his crimes against the state. Despite his success in building the **Great City of Wu**, which still exists as Suzhou today, and his military leadership that allowed Wu to become a dominant state at the end of the Spring and Autumn Period, his life ended in disgrace. His lifeless body was then rolled into the river, where it washed away in the current.

Some sources say that Wu Zixu, prior to committing suicide, asked King Fuchai to remove his eyes and hang them on the gates of the city so he could watch as the Yue destroyed the state of Wu. This would end up being a prophetic statement.

It would later turn out that Bo Pi had been working with the Yue behind the king's back and had accepted several bribes to divert the king's attention away from the state of Yue, which planned to annex Wu and gain control of their territory and people. Just as Wu Zixu predicted, the Yue attacked the Wu in 473 BCE, annexing the state and ending Wu's reign as a superpower and as an individual state.

King Fuchai regretted not listening to Wu Zixu, but it was too late. With no recourse left, King Fuchai committed suicide as the Yue took control of his kingdom. But first, he covered his face, so he wouldn't have to face Wu Zixu in the afterlife.

Wu Zixu is remembered in a memorial built in Suzhou in 2004. His image and name are still relevant in contemporary Chinese culture. There are various plays, operas, and poems about him. Some people in China worship him as a river god, or "god of the waves." In fact, some people believe that the origin of the traditional holiday of the Dragon Boat Festival (also called the Duanwu Festival) commemorates Wu Zixu's death as he was thrown into the river near the Great City, Suzhou.

The Chu State

According to *The Records of the Grand Historian*, the rulers of the Chu State were directly descended from the Yellow Emperor, also called the "Yellow Deity."

中央黃帝

The Yellow Emperor is considered both a historical and mythological figure in Chinese culture.

Prior to King Zhao of the Zhou Dynasty's rule, the Chu were independently governed but had been on good terms with the Zhou Dynasty for centuries. However, during the time of Zhao, tensions began to build between the two. Chu controlled a mineral-rich area, and the need for copper and tin drove the king to expand his boundaries into the Yangtze basin, subduing the Han states and initially overtaking Chu. Chu, however, continued to expand their boundaries north, and King Zhao perceived this as defiance. He could not retain control over the area, so in 977 BCE, King Zhao led a military campaign against the Confederation of Chu, but drowned in the Han River before he reached them. This badly damaged the Zhou Dynasty's image, marking the end of the Western Zhou Period and beginning the Spring and Autumn Period.

This allowed the Chu to gain independence much faster than the states to the north, because they lived so far away from the centralized power, and because they had shown they could not be controlled by the powerful Zhou Dynasty. This strengthened Chu forces and bolstered their morale, causing them to increase their expansionist principles.

Even in the peaceful early years of the Spring and Autumn Period, Chu was engaged in conquest. They had a strong military and began to conquer the smaller states around them, notably the state of E in 863 BCE. By 703 BCE, Xiong Tong declared himself king and established Chu as an independent kingdom. They were even considered one of the five hegemons during the Hegemon Era.

Because they were so focused on outward expansion, many alliances were formed to counteract the Chu's greed for land and power between their rival states. After the Jin allied with the Wu to defeat the Chu, the Chu king Zhao was forced to flee the capital twice because of the invading Wu. The Wu, who for the first time rivaled their power in the south, became the first real adversary of the Chu, who eventually partnered with the Yue to defeat the Wu.

While the Wu were initially able to defeat the Chu and Yue forces, the partnership resulted in the Chu providing resources and training for the Yue, which eventually allowed them to overtake and annex the state of Wu.

After the Wu were defeated, Chu began to rapidly expand again. In 479 BCE, they annexed Chen; in 449 BCE, they overtook Cai. Despite these power grabs, the Chu didn't return to the fierce nation that they were before the Wu-Chu Wars for many years, and they were eventually defeated by the Qin, who became the next ruling dynasty of China.

Corruption and extravagance overtook the Chu state by the end of the fifth century BCE, and King Dao made Wu Qi his chancellor. Wu Qi instituted reforms to rein in spending and rid the state of useless or corrupt officials. Under Wu Qi's guidance, the Chu were able to reform their armies and return the Chu state to a position of power. In 334 BCE, the Chu defeated and overtook the Yue state, and Yue was split between the Chu and Qi. They controlled more land than any other state at this point, almost a third of the total landmass of ancient China. As they expanded outward, they once again became a formidable force. Despite his effective reform of the Chu state, Wu Qi remained unpopular with the people of Chu and was assassinated at King Dao's funeral.

While Wu Qi was one of the prominent forces in Chu in the Warring States Period, he is most remembered for his military treatise. Wu Qi's book, *The Book of Master Wu*, or *Wuzi*, is one of the seven military classics of China, along with *The Art of War*.

His military intelligence certainly helped the Chu state to expand, and effectively defeat their enemies, prior to his assassination.

In 241 BCE, five states formed an alliance to fight against pressure from the Qin, who were steadily annexing the land and people around their state. Those states were: Chu, Zhao, Wei, Yan, and Han. They attacked the Qin but were defeated, despite their careful planning and superior tactical position. Some states, such as the state of Han, surrendered rather than continue to fight the formidable Qin. The Chu moved their capital to a point farther away from Qin's advances. In 278 BCE, the Qin took the former capital city of Ying and began making their way toward the new capital of Shanzou.

As the Qin advanced, the Chu were forced to expand to the south and east, the borders that were farthest away from the invading Qin. While they managed to continue their expansion in these directions, the Qin began to move deeper into Chu territory from the other side. The country could no longer sustain a policy of moving their boundaries and chose instead to aggressively defend themselves from the Qin. But it was too late.

They were the second-to-last state to fall to the Qin, and only the Qi held out longer before eventually falling in 221 BCE. This marked the end of the Zhou Dynasty as well as the beginning of the Qin Dynasty.

Five Hegemons

In the early Spring and Autumn Period, the Zhou Kingdom was made of hundreds of small states, all vying for power and control in their respective regions. Strong states annexed weak ones early in the period, and contended for what is called hegemony, or dominance, over all the others. During this period, five states would emerge as powerful leaders; Qi, Song, Jin, Qin, and Chu.

Duke Huan of Qi, Duke Wen of Jin, Duke Xiang of Song, Duke Mu of Qin, and King Zhuang of Chu became the hegemons and were called the "Five Powers of the Spring and Autumn Period." Some historians remove Qin and Song from this list and use King Helu of Wu and King Goujian of Yue in their stead.

The hegemons of this time were expected to keep stability among those they presided over and uphold the framework of the entire system of interstate relations. They often protected a series of smaller surrounding states who, in turn, became subjects of the hegemon and paid tribute to that leader in return for the stability they were provided.

The Warring States Period

While the Battle of Baiju took place during the Spring and Autumn Period, and while Sun Tzu probably didn't live long enough to see the beginning of the Warring States Period, the Battle of Baiju had a profound impact on the Warring States Period that came shortly after his demise.

The quest for expansion that happened in the Chu state, which led to the years of warring with their border neighbors, set the stage for this period, which is marked by political unrest, violence, and quests for control of the entirety of China. Many states began to expand their borders, slowly annexing and enveloping the smaller states around them. As the small states were overtaken and combined, only seven states would remain, all of which were superpowers during the Warring States Period. Whether they were interested in simply surviving as independent kingdoms, or

Shang Yang implemented many reforms using the ideas of Chinese legalism.

if their interest lay in overthrowing the Zhou and eventually controlling all of the states of ancient China, states at this time spent countless resources on the development of super-strong armies. For the first half of the Warring States Period, the boundaries of the superpowers changed very little, but as time went on, the battles grew bloodier, and violence erupted constantly between neighboring states. Many states, like the Wu at the end of the Spring and Autumn Period, found that they were fighting a battle on every border, trying to maintain control over their own land or to invade their neighboring states to annex them.

In 361 BCE, a man named Shang Yang came to power in the court system in Qin, and for the next two decades, he would enact changes that entirely changed the way courts acted in bureaucratic affairs. Shang Yang's ideas, implemented through law and policy, carried sweeping changes that would set the stage for the Qin to ignore former military etiquette and become ruthless warriors.

They would go on to run their state, and later their dynasty, from a point of tight central control, exhibited through grand shows of power on the part of the state. Yang Shang not only implemented systems of rewards for farmers who exceeded harvest expectations, but used crop surpluses to attain wealth for the state that could be applied to military spending and public works projects. He enslaved those farmers who had poor yields, sentencing them to work on infrastructure projects like roadways and canals, which improved the mobility of the troops, once deployed, to conquer their neighbor states. His ideas were from the philosophy of **legalism,** and they had a profound effect on the future of China both during and beyond the Warring States Period.

Legalism

There are six "classical schools of thought" in Chinese culture, and one of those is legalism. Legalism is credited to Han Fei (Han Feizi) in the third century BCE, who drew largely on the teaching of Shang Yang during the Warring States Period. While it contains no moral code as Confucianism and Taoism do, though they were all created around the same time, it does lay out a system for government that was instrumental not just in the Qin Dynasty, but through Chinese history.

One of the major changes under legalist philosophy is that everyone should be evaluated on an even keel, and that people should all be considered in the same way. This was very different than the eras leading up to the Qin Dynasty, in which kinship and family lines were valued over talent. This idea of bureaucracy over familial leadership allowed government officials to be hired for their skill instead of for their royal blood, meaning that Qin, who practiced legalism and its ideas, had a more talented army and more skilled government officials in the Warring States Period than many of the neighboring states.

Legalism also presupposes that people are more inclined to do wrong than right, and that human nature causes people to act in ways that are violent and chaotic instead of noble and kind. Shang Yang lived during a time when war was a daily reality for many people, and this meant that often the side of human nature that people experienced was ruthless and cruel. The thought process was that people are inherently selfish: they kill, steal, lie, and cheat if it is in their best interest, unless an external force keeps them from committing these acts. The state needs to act as that force, and by implementing fixed, transparent rules, and enacting immediate punishment, the state can impose a system of proper behavior. Many legalist theorists went even beyond this, privileging rules and laws over leadership, and believing that in a perfect state there would be no need for a leader because the laws would cause people to behave. Legalism imposes a system of strict and severe punishment for those who break laws and the threat of punitive action to keep people in line.

Not only was this applied to the people within the Qin state, but the Qin dealt with large-scale insurrection in the same way. Any uprising or attempt at attack from another state was met with severe and immediate retribution. By dismissing former ideas of chivalry and justice in war, and fully committing to quelling any dissent, they could fully crush their enemies.

During the Qin Dynasty, legalism became the official state philosophy, even in times of peace. Subjects of the Qin were sentenced to harsh penalties and fines for even minor offenses. Many of the people who completed the grueling labor of building the **Great Wall of China** were sentenced to do so by the courts in payment for their crimes.

The Great Wall of China was built by many slaves sentenced to hard labor for crimes against the state.

During the Han Dynasty, legalism was eventually outlawed in favor of Confucianism, though legalism would intermittently resurface in times of peril. This was especially true when the Chinese felt they were losing the control of the people. **Mao Zedong** notably used a form of legalism to restructure China, hailing it as a progressive policy, between 1949 and 1976.

Qin Dynasty

While the Qin Dynasty was the briefest in duration of any dynasty in Chinese history, they accomplished a lot during their reign from 221–206 BCE.

At the end of the Warring States Period, when all of the seven states had fallen except one, the Qin became the next ruling dynasty. After their victory, they unified China for the first time under a single central government without feudal states. By ruling from a central government instead of using the Fenfeng System, they were able to consolidate resources and impose a unified legal system throughout all of the former states. The lesson learned from the end of the Spring and Autumn Period, and throughout the Warring States Period, was that giving individual rulers too much authority or autonomy would lead to insurrection.

The leader of the Qin, Ying Zheng, did not call himself king once his rule was established over the area that had formerly been made up of several smaller states, instead opting for the term emperor. After declaring himself the emperor, he also changed his name, henceforth being known as **Shi Huangti** (Qin Shi Huang).

By setting up a strong centralized government, the Qin strengthened their economy, allowing the state to support a large army. By implementing the same rules and laws throughout their land, they were able to regulate many aspects of daily life that were formerly ignored. The Qin Dynasty made lasting changes in Chinese culture by establishing a state currency, standardizing weights and measures for the entire empire, and creating a state-sponsored written language so that people from different clans and backgrounds all used the same characters.

Under the Qin, dissent was not only discouraged, but illegal. The severe punishments for crimes included castration, and many **eunuchs** were then enslaved. In fact, much of the

Terracotta Army was likely made by eunuch slaves of the Qin Empire. Eunuchs were considered to make superior servants in the era by being removed from sexuality and distraction. Many men were also castrated prior to puberty in order to go into the service of the king or emperor. As a result of purpose and punishment, many eunuchs lived in the Chinese empire during the Qin Dynasty.

Due to the severity with which he ruled, Shi Huangti had frequent assassination attempts made on his life. Because of this, he grew increasingly paranoid and began to obsessively search for an elixir that would grant him immortality. On one trip to the far eastern reaches of his kingdom, where Taoist magicians promised such an elixir was being guarded by sea monsters on a secluded island, he died. Ironically, he was killed by the mercury used in an elixir meant to induce immortality. He died without naming a successor.

His advisors then conspired to stop the emperor's eldest son, Fusu, who was the rightful heir without any written will stating otherwise, from taking the throne. Shi Huangti's advisor Li Si and the chief eunuch Zhao Gao feared that if Fusu was enthroned, they would lose their standing. They forged a letter from Qin Shi Huang saying that Fusu should commit suicide, and their plan worked. The emperor's younger son Huhui, later known by Qin Er Shi, then ascended the throne.

He was not as capable as his father and even more ruthless than his predecessors had been. He ruled by executing many people, raising taxes to unpayable levels, arresting messengers who brought bad news, and committing to unnecessary public works projects such as lacquering all the walls of the kingdom. The people of the empire began to revolt, and Huhui was forced to commit suicide. His nephew, who ascended the throne afterward, was quickly defeated by Chu rebels and executed.

Shi Huangti (also known as Shi Huangdi or Qin Shi Huang) first unified the states of China in 221 BCE, marking the start of the Qin Dynasty.

Despite the short duration of their rule, the name Qin (pronounced 'Chin') is probably what gives modern-day China its name.

Han Dynasty

The Chu and Han States battled for control of newly unified China at the end of the Qin Dynasty. The Battle of Gaixia was the turning point; after this battle, the Chu were defeated and the Han Dynasty rose to claim the emperorship from the Qin.

The Han were not so far removed from the Warring States Period, and as such, were highly influenced by the times. They retained the bureaucratic structures favored by the Qin and a central government to rule the people. While they also maintained the idea of fixed, transparent laws, they did not rule with such severity as their Qin predecessors.

The Han Dynasty successfully quelled rebellions for the majority of their rule, despite a small interruption in the middle of their reign, and even expanded the empire by conquering new land in the Tamin basin.

In the beginning of the Han Dynasty, they kept a gentler form of legalism as their state policy, which would eventually give way to Confucianism as the official state philosophy. They then made it illegal for anyone to follow the teachings of Han Fei or Shang Yang, attacking those who were loyal to those philosophies in much the same way the Qin had disavowed Confucianism and Taoism. The form of Confucianism that the Han used was a mixture of legalism and Confucianism based on the writings of Xunzi, who taught that human nature was evil, and Mencius, who believed humans were basically good but needed thorough training to retain moral lessons. This was unusual, as Confucius

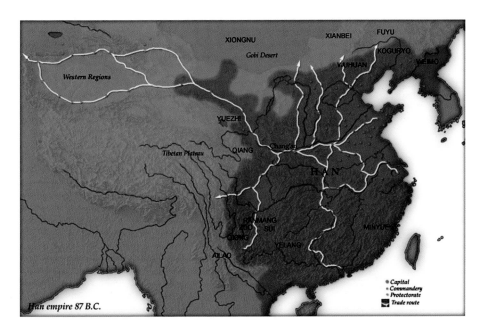

The Han Dynasty greatly expanded the land area of China during their rule.

taught of the natural goodness in people. These ideas, however, helped the Han justify their rule while giving the people of the kingdom a more inclusive state philosophy that allowed them more autonomy.

CHAPTER FIVE

Myths, Legends, *and* Popular Culture

Although we may never know if Sun Tzu actually existed, the work *The Art of War* continues to be one of the most important books of all time. It still sells millions of copies each year and has been adapted to suit a range of professions, teaching wisdom and problem-solving to generation after generation of people. Though the book is available for free (all books published before 1923 in the United States have become public domain), it continues to be a bestseller nationwide.

Prominent Military Figures Who Used *The Art of War*

The lessons contained within *The Art of War* have influenced people since the Spring and Autumn Period, in which it was (likely) written. During the Warring States Period, when most

Opposite: Bound bamboo slips like these were used to make books, such as *The Art of War*, in ancient China.

generals read and applied the lessons in the text to their battles with neighboring states, they must have guessed that the book was powerful. The first emperor of the Qin Dynasty credited the book for the end of the Warring States Period and his ability to gain control of China. But it may have been beyond their wildest dreams to assume that more than 2,000 years later, it would still be widely read around the entire world!

Japan was introduced to the book by the eighth century, and many generals there quickly took to it. It played a key role in unifying Japan, just as it had in China. Takeda Shingen (1521–1573) was said to be "nearly invincible" on the battlefield because he religiously applied the concepts in the text to his battles, and his "Wind, Forest, Fire and Mountain" strategy was an evolution of the precepts laid forth by Sun Tzu, as Sun Tzu taught soldiers to, "Move swift as the Wind and closely-formed as the Wood. Attack like the Fire and be still as the Mountain." Even the **samurai**, famed warriors of Japan, were known to have studied and honored the teachings in the text, and used them to further develop their distinct style of combat. Much later in history, there were accounts of the admiral of the fleet who led Japan's forces to victory against Russia in the Russo-Japanese War, having applied the ideas in *The Art of War* to his naval strategy.

When a French Jesuit missionary named Joseph Amiot came into contact with the book in the 1770s, it was widely read in Asia but still unknown to the Western world. The missionary brought a copy of the text back to France and had it translated and published there. It quickly won regard with many French leaders, especially Napoleon Bonaparte. Napoleon found much success by applying Sun Tzu's idea of Chang and Ch'i—a direct attack followed by a smaller surprise attack—in his conquests in Europe. Unfortunately, Napoleon did not pay attention to the

Skilled Japanese warriors, called samurai, often adhered to practices from *The Art of War*.

chapters on maintaining position, which would have saved him from a bitter loss to the Russians at the end of his reign. Many subsequent European rulers would use Sun Tzu as an inspiration and guide when going into war.

In the mid-twentieth century, Mao Zedong (Tse-tung) said this his victory over Chiang Kai-shek was owed to Sun Tzu, whose text he studied. Mao used the ideas in the book to effectively change the country over to a communist state, as it remains today. Another prominent Communist leader, Joseph Stalin of Russia, also read *The Art of War* and applied those techniques to his strategy when facing Adolf Hitler and Nazi Germany in World War II. While Joseph Stalin is frequently criticized for his paranoia and harsh treatment of the Russian people at the end of his tenure, and he certainly did some terrible things, he was instrumental in stopping the Nazis from invading more countries in Europe, possibly even conquering the entire continent. Sun Tzu provided him with at least some of the knowledge he needed to fight back against the Nazi regime even as the capital city, Leningrad (formerly known as Saint Petersburg), was under siege by German troops for 872 days. Using the principles in *The Art of War*, Stalin reestablished control over the Soviet Union and effectively freed Europe from occupation by Nazi forces.

While *The Art of War* was published in English as early as 1905 (which is late considering the longevity of the book beforehand), nothing brought it to the attention of American military men like the Vietnam War. General Vo Nguyen Giap, one of Vietnam's formidable military leaders, directly applied many of Sun Tzu's teachings and was able to lead the Vietcong to victory, despite the resources and weaponry of the American and French forces they were facing. American soldiers in Vietnam were challenged, and consistently defeated, by generals who were said to be able to recite whole passages from the book by memory. The book is now a part of the Marine Corps Professional Reading Program, recommended reading for all US intelligence officers, and required reading for CIA personnel. In the 1990s, the American study of the book was put to the test during the Gulf War. General Norman Schwarzkopf and General Colin Powell both used Sun Tzu's principles, mainly deception, speed, and attacking the enemy's weaknesses, to quickly achieve victory.

Lessons From *The Art of War*

Interestingly, the major lessons in *The Art of War* are how to avoid actual warfare—unless it is of absolute necessity. While Sima Qian paints a picture of Sun Tzu as a ruthless man in the story of the concubines, many of the ideas in the texts are actually intended to maintain peace. In fact, Sun Tzu even goes so far as to say, "The greatest victory is that which requires no battle."

The thirteen chapters in the book each correspond to an important lesson. In order, they are: Laying Plans, Waging War, The Plan of Attack, Positioning, Directing, Weak Points and Strong, Maneuvering, The Nine Variations, The Army on the March, Terrain, The Nine Terrains, Attack by Fire, and The Use of Spies. Each of these lessons provides an in-depth look at that facet of war with examples, insight, and strategies for achievement.

Many of the lessons contained in the text closely mirror the ideas of Taoism. For instance, according to Sun Tzu, the five most virtuous attributes are wisdom, sincerity, benevolence, discipline, and courage. These closely mirror the virtues outlined in Taoism, as well as Confucianism. Like Lao Tzu, Sun Tzu advocates abstaining from war and quelling battles with deception and strategy before they begin. Much of the book is dedicated to

Phil Jackson is one of many coaches who uses lessons from *The Art of War* in athletics.

ATHLETICS AND *THE ART OF WAR*

Many military strategists have used *The Art of War* for military purposes throughout the years, but many people have applied the principles outlined in the book to various arenas of life. Even American sports teams have benefited from the strategies outlined in the book. Many coaches in the United States use the book to plan for "battles" on the field or in the arena and have achieved many victories for the teams they lead.

One such person is Bill Belichick, head coach for the National Football League's New England Patriots. Belichick has professed his fondness for the book, citing the art of deception and knowing your enemy as vital components to defeating your opponents. Under Belichick, the New England Patriots have been wildly successful, claiming several conference championships and winning four Super Bowls.

Bill Walsh, the coach of another NFL team, the San Francisco 49ers, also claimed *The Art of War* helped him achieve success on the field. Using the principles of Sun Tzu, he was able to take a football team who had only won two games the season before he started coaching, all the way to the Super Bowl just two years later.

National Basketball Association (NBA) coach Phil Jackson also used the text to create strategies for his basketball team. As head coach of the Chicago Bulls, he took the team to six championships in nine years. When he was head coach of the Los Angeles Lakers, the team won five championships in ten years. He currently holds the record for the most championships (as a coach) in the history of the NBA. He is also the only coach to have ever won multiple championships with more than one team.

In addition to American athletics, the book is used worldwide by many other coaches in a variety of sports. For example, Luiz Felipe Scolari calls himself a devotee of the book and led Brazil to victory in the World Cup in Soccer in 2002. Robbie Deans, the Australian Rugby coach, also uses it.

In recent years, there have even been books published about how to use *The Art of War* to succeed in athletic events. Because so many sports mimic battles, the advice is nearly a one-to-one correspondence.

keeping peace, and those parts dedicated to war advocate ending battles quickly and efficiently because war, they both believed, was damaging to both sides—even the victor. Sun Tzu even wrote of the life force, "the way," that Taoists believe is the basis for all things. In fact, when naming the "five fundamental factors" that must be considered in battle, he lists Tao first. The following four are heaven, earth, command, and rules.

Because the lessons in the book extend beyond just battle, many of the sayings from the text have become popular quotes in contemporary society. Many of the sayings have been applied indiscriminately to other aspects of life, and people are unaware that Sun Tzu was the original author. One example of this is his, "Appear weak when you are strong, and strong when you are weak." This quote applies to many situations beyond war: the death of a loved one, a break-up, or even a sporting event can benefit from the root meaning of this phrase.

Due to the human, relatable nature of many of the lessons in the text, the book has been overhauled to provide advice for a number of situations. You can buy dating books that apply the principles of *The Art of War* to romantic relationships and the pursuit of a perfect mate. There are books that apply Sun Tzu's teachings to politics, law, athletics, and even parenting.

A recent boom industry has been created around business books based on *The Art of War*. Economists, CEOs, and marketing firms have all been drawn to the book because the principles can be easily applied to almost any facet of the business world. In addition to countless articles written about applying Sun Tzu's tactics to business published by major companies like *Forbes* and *Business Insider*, no less than a dozen books explaining how to use *The Art of War* in business fields have been published over the last several years. Larry Ellison, the brash CEO of Oracle and one of the more successful businessmen of our time, claims he personally adheres to Sun Tzu's teaching in both business and life. He believes that much of his success is attributed to his study of the book.

Martial Arts

Martial arts in America have evolved from traditions and combat practices over centuries (though some are newer forms of older practices). They may or may not involve striking, kicking, weaponry, or grappling as part of their practice. Several martial arts are quite popular in the United States today, including karate, judo, and aikido.

Chinese martial arts originated several millennia ago in the Xia Dynasty. The Yellow Emperor of China is credited with introducing these fighting techniques to the people of China, though the tradition of folklore that provides such information is not always credible.

While martial arts existed in China for many centuries before the Warring States Period, it was during this time that hand-to-hand combat techniques became a priority for warriors. Because weapons were expensive and could not be mass-produced, it was rare for a soldier to have a high quality weapon of his own, even if he were going into battle as part of a large army. The weapons that were available during this time were heavy and unwieldy, making them problematic on a battlefield. Being able to subdue an enemy with your bare hands was very important for soldiers of the era, and many new techniques arose during this time. There are more than sixty distinct styles of martial arts practiced in the Chinese tradition, often falling under the umbrella term **kung fu** in American practice.

Many martial arts, such as kung fu, have principles based in the teachings of Sun Tzu.

The basis for many of these new techniques was *The Art of War* and the teachings of Sun Tzu, along with the *Tao Te Ching* and *Zhuangzi*. Most of the principles of contemporary martial arts grew from methods described in his military treatise. The idea of martial arts is to train one's whole being to respond to conflict, with body, emotion, and mind all working together. While martial arts involves physical strength and commitment, and conditioning is common, the training of the mind through meditation and careful thought processes is equally important for mastery. Sun Tzu explained this concept by exposing illusion of power versus real strength. By using your opponent's weaknesses against them, even a smaller person can defeat a larger rival.

Pop Culture

The Art of War has not only remained popular for readers, but it has also been used by media as a go-to character reference for many fictional characters. It has been used in television and movies in recent history as a display of character strength or as a precursor to battle.

Whether or not it is intentional, *Star Wars* creator George Lucas took the idea of "the way" from Sun Tzu's *The Art of War* and Lao-Tzu's *Tao Te Ching* and transformed it into "the force"— the underlying life force that drives the warriors of the Jedi and the Sith. This has led to countless fan pages being overrun with comparisons between the force and the Taoist religion.

Another example is the 1987 movie *Wall Street,* directed by Oliver Stone. The two main characters, Bud Fox and Gordon Gekko, who are involved in an underhanded business deal, both mention the book. The movie greatly increased the book's popularity, and many people released versions of the text around

The Art of War was featured in the popular television series
The Sopranos.

this time, trying to capitalize on the sudden bump in sales the
movie caused.

In 1999, the wildly popular HBO television show *The
Sopranos* also mentioned *The Art of War*. The main character,
Tony Soprano, was the head of a Mafia family in New Jersey.
He points out the relevance of the book to his therapist, after
she recommends the book to him. He quotes it, explaining how
information relates to his strategy as a mob boss. This also caused
a considerable bump in sales of the book, causing a new rash of
versions to hit the book market in the early 2000s.

In the year 2000, a movie titled *The Art of War* greatly benefited from the book's recent success. Though the movie was not related to the book in any way, except that it was set in China, it achieved moderate success by exploiting the title of the popular military text.

In 2002, *James Bond: Die Another Day* used *The Art of War* when developing their villain. Though the mention is brief, the North Korean foe is said to be a student of Sun Tzu's work. In one scene, a character is stabbed with a knife that had been stuck into a copy of *The Art of War*.

Sun Tzu himself has also been used as a character in fictional works—perhaps most notably in the forty-part historical drama series *Bing Sheng*. This docudrama takes place in ancient China and focuses on the life of Sun Tzu (played by Zhu Yawen), exploring life during the Spring and Autumn Period and recreating historic battles such as the Battle of Baiju to give a realistic glimpse of what Sun Tzu might have been like and how his life unfolded. There have also been several in-depth documentaries produced about Sun Tzu and *The Art of War,* showing that despite the book's age, it is still relevant and fascinating to people today.

Lionel Giles and the Legacy of Translation

The most popular version of the book sold today was translated and compiled by Lionel Giles, a British Scholar and Assistant Curator at the British Museum. In addition to his scholarly pursuits, he also spoke several languages and acted as a translator and the Keeper of the Department of Oriental Manuscripts for the museum.

Lionel's father, Herbert Giles, was a prominent **sinologist** and professor at Cambridge. He was also one of the two developers of the **Wade-Giles Romanization** method for translating Chinese into written English, which is the form that Lionel used when translating *The Art of War*. His father's interest in the language and culture seem to have taken hold in his son, who continued in the fields of history and sinology like his father before him.

After reading the untranslated text from China and upon reading the first English-language version published just a few years before, Lionel Giles decided that he needed to republish the work with a more accurate translation. He heavily criticized the version of *The Art of War* that had been published in English in 1905, noting that it didn't match the original text in any meaningful way. He said of the work, "Omissions were frequent; hard passages were willfully distorted or slurred over." Lionel released his version just five years later, in 1910.

Though much time has passed since Lionel Giles published his version of *The Art of War*, it has held up well. He also translated a series of other Chinese texts, including the *Tao Te Ching* and the *Analects of Confucius*. He is often praised for his use of Chinese idiom, elegant sparse language, and ability to mirror the Chinese style of writing in his English translations. He even manages some rhymed jingles that stay true to the original intent as well as the original form of the text.

His introduction to *The Art of War* is praised for the dedicated accuracy with which he presents what he knows of Sun Tzu. His dogged attempts at setting the stage give the reader background on the era and the culture before examining historical mention of the author in other works. No other version of the book presents such a scholarly look at the timeframe within which the book was written, nor do they carry the copious notes of Giles's translation.

While this is still the most common translation available, that does not mean it is without fault. Some have criticized the book as less accessible than other translations. Later versions by Samuel B. Griffith (1963) and Thomas Cleary (1988) are considered more lucid, and are considered to be very good translations of the original work by scholars.

Conclusions

Any name that survives in history for 2,400 years, such as Sun Tzu, is a name worth knowing. Sun Tzu changed the course of history, both in the era in which he lived and even in modern times. In addition to providing a text that has been so invaluable to people all over the world, Sun Tzu also presents something more interesting; a mystery.

The man behind the legend may have been an ordinary man. However, the legend is far-reaching and inspires courage and focus in many. Unlike the many kings and dukes we remember as historical figures from a bygone era, relics of the Spring and Autumn or Warring States Periods, Sun Tzu feels alive. Reading his words, you can imagine he is speaking directly to you. The legends, as well as the advice contained in *The Art of War,* allow us to experience Sun Tzu as both a celebrity and a friend, both inspiring and intimate. He left us a living piece of history to look to in uncertain times. He isn't just a name written in a history book, or an author listed on the copyright page of a military treatise, but a cause for excitement. Sun Tzu truly changed the world, but more importantly, he shows us that we can, too.

CHRONOLOGY

8,000–6,500 BCE Peasants begin to settle in the Yangtze River Valley. the first record of rice being farmed

2698–2598 BCE The mythical rule of the Yellow Emperor

2070 BCE The Xia Dynasty begins

1700 BCE Chariots are introduced to the Chinese by the tribes of the Eurasian Steppes (some historians date this closer to 1300 BCE)

1600 BCE Xia Dynasty ends; Shang Dynasty begins

1046 BCE Shang Dynasty ends; Zhou Dynasty begins

771 BCE Spring and Autumn Period begins

551 BCE Confucius is born

544 BCE Sun Tzu is born

514 BCE King Helu ascends the throne in Wu after having his cousin assassinated

512 BCE Wu-Chu Wars begin

510 BCE Sun Tzu completes *The Art of War;* King Helu appoints Sun Tzu a general in Wu's army

506 BCE Battle of Baiju

496 BCE King Helu and Sun Tzu die

484 BCE Wu Zixu is forced to commit suicide

479 BCE Confucius dies

475 BCE Warring States Period begins

473 BCE The Wu are defeated and annexed by the Yue

464 BCE The last year of history covered in the *Zuo Zhuan*

338 BCE Death of Shang Yang

328 BCE The state of Qin begins to take control of China by conquering the states surrounding them

221 BCE Zhou Dynasty ends; Qin Dynasty begins

220 BCE Construction on the "Northern Wall" expands, and it becomes The Great Wall of China

206 BCE Qin Dynasty ends; Han dynasty begins

800 CE *The Art of War* becomes popular in Japan

1782 CE *The Art of War* is translated into French by a Jesuit missionary

1905 CE The first English-language translation of *The Art of War* is published

1910 CE Lionel Giles translates *The Art of War* and publishes his own version of the treatise

1987 CE The movie *Wall Street* repopularizes *The Art of War* in the United States

GLOSSARY

BATTLE OF BAIJU (BOJU) Wu's victory against the Chu, led by King Helu, Wu Zixu, and Sun Tzu.

BATTLE OF MUYE The battle between the Shang and the Zhou that effectively ended the Shang Dynasty and ushered in the beginning of the Zhou Dynasty.

CHARIOT A wheeled, horse-drawn cart used for moving quickly, particularly in battle.

CONCUBINE A woman who lives with a man but has lower household status than his wife or wives.

COURTESY NAME A name which one is known by for professional or formal purposes.

CUIRASS Armor that consists of a breastplate and backplate that fasten together.

DAGGER-AXE A long-handled weapon mounted with a dagger head, an ax head, a spear head, or any combination of the three.

EUNUCH A castrated male servant.

FENGJIAN (FENFANG) SYSTEM A feudal system of dividing land among rulers who in turn pay tribute to a central king.

FEUDALISM A political or social system of land ownership and stratification in society.

FOUR BOOKS AND FIVE CLASSICS The classic books of China, mostly written or edited by Confucius.

FOUR OCCUPATIONS The four types of people; scholars, farmers, craftsmen, and merchants.

GONGZHENG A high-ranking officer that oversees the production of craftsmen and artisans.

GREAT CITY OF WU Modern day Suzhou; the city that would tie celestial and earth attributes together designed by Wu Zixu under King Helu.

GREAT WALL OF CHINA A wall in Northern China constructed as early as the Zhou dynasty to keep northern "barbarians" out of China.

HEGEMON A powerful entity, in this case a state in China, that is a social and political leader for the region.

HISTORICITY The idea of whether or not something is historically accurate, or if a person really existed.

KING HELU The King of Wu who appointed Sun Tzu as a general and used his strategy to defeat the Chu.

KUNG FU An umbrella term for the many schools of martial arts in China.

LIONEL GILES Translator of the most popular translation of *The Art of War* in 1910.

MANDATE OF HEAVEN The idea that whoever currently had power was chosen to rule by the gods.

MAO ZEDONG The communist leader of China from 1948–1976. Known for producing a little red book of wisdom that many people carried with them during his rule.

ONE HUNDRED SCHOOLS OF THOUGHT Descriptive of the era in which philosophy and independent thought flourished in China, during the Spring and Autumn Period.

SAMURAI A secretive, skilled warrior of Japanese origin, known for their distinctive face masks and armor and their fierce style in battle.

SEVEN WARRING STATES The states that remained in the Warring States Period, who were always at war with one another.

SHI HUANGTI The first Emperor of the Qin Dynasty, who effectively unified the seven states in his short dynastic rules.

SINOLOGIST A Western historian who engages in the study of China or "the Orient."

SPRING AND AUTUMN PERIOD The period in the middle of the Zhou Dynasty, known for the seeds of political unrest and moral scholarship.

SUN BIN Possibly the grandson of Sun Tzu. He wrote a second *Art of War*, which is also considered to be an important military text.

TERRACOTTA ARMY A set of 8,000 or more life-sized soldiers constructed from terracotta and buried with Shi Huangti.

TREBUCHET A sling weapon that used gravity or man power to fling objects at enemy forces.

WADE-GILES ROMANIZATION A specific way of translating Chinese into English by using a system that mimics the sound of Chinese speech.

WESTERN ZHOU The first part of the Zhou Dynasty; considered a golden age for China.

WU-CHU WARS A series of battles fought between the Wu and Chu states at the end of the Spring and Autumn Period.

WU ZIXU King Helu's chief advisor, who aided the king in assassinating his cousin and ascending the throne before introducing him to Sun Tzu and helping him defeat the Chu.

YELLOW EMPEROR Probably, though not definitely, a mythical figure who is said to be the first ruler of China. He is also called the "Yellow Deity," and one of his wives is also worshipped for discovering silk.

FURTHER INFORMATION

BOOKS

Buckley Ebrey, Patricia. *The Cambridge Illustrated History of China*. Cambridge University Press: 2010.

The Editorial Committee of Chinese. *China: Five Thousand Years of History and Civilization*. City University of Hong Kong: 2007.

Tzu, Sun and Giles, Lionel. *The Art of War*. Cosimo Classics (Reprint): 2010.

WEBSITES

Discovery Education: Lesson Plan Library

http://www.discoveryeducation.com/teachers/free-lesson-plans/the-art-of-war.cfm

Lesson plans and resources for teaching *The Art of War*.

History of China

http://www.chaos.umd.edu/history/toc.html

A comprehensive database with links to articles on different periods in China's history.

National Geographic

http://science.nationalgeographic.com/science/archaeology/emperor-qin/

Photos and information about the Terracotta Army.

Sun Tzu

http://www.history.com/topics/sun-tzu

A biography of Sun Tzu with relevant cultural information.

TES USA

https://www.tes.com/teaching-resource/the-art-of-war-by-sun-tzu-6231903

Links to a free, downloadable copy of *The Art of War* from Project Gutenberg.

VIDEOS

Ask HISTORY: Can You See the Great Wall From Space?

http://www.history.com/topics/great-wall-of-china/videos

A visual history of The Great Wall of China from *National Geographic*.

Chinese History: The Zhou Dynasty

https://www.youtube.com/watch?v=EkNMZoHlUzw

A concise video history of the Zhou Dynasty.

BIBLIOGRAPHY

Carruthers, Bob, trans. *Sun Tzu: The Art of War: The Illustrated Edition*. Barnsley: Pen & Sword Military, 2013.

Ebrey, Patricia Buckley. *The Cambridge Illustrated History of China*. Cambridge: Cambridge University Press, 1999.

History.com Staff. "The Art of War." History.com. 2010. http://www.history.com/topics/the-art-of-war.

Hui, Victoria Tin-bor. *War and State Formation in Ancient China and Early Modern Europe*. New York NY: Cambridge University Press, 2005.

Lau, D.C. and Roger T. Ames. *Sun Bin: The Art of Warfare: A Translation of the Classic Chinese Work of Philosophy and Strategy*. Albany: State University of New York Press, 2003.

Mark, Emily. "Legalism." *Ancient History Encyclopedia*. Last modified January 31, 2016. http://www.ancient.eu/Legalism/.

Mark, Joshua J. "Ancient China." *Ancient History Encyclopedia*. Last modified December 18, 2012. http://www.ancient.eu/china/.

Mark, Joshua J. "Sun-Tzu." *Ancient History Encyclopedia*. Last modified January 04, 2013. http://www.ancient.eu/Sun-Tzu/.

Nylan, Michael. *The Five "Confucian" Classics*. New Haven: Yale University Press, 2001.

Science of Strategy Institute. "The Nine Formulas of Sun Tzu's *The Art of War*." Accessed December 05, 2016. http://scienceofstrategy.org/main/content/sun-tzu-successes-public-sphere.

Sima, Qian, and Burton Watson. *Records of the Grand Historian*. Hong Kong: Columbia University Press, 1993.

Sunzi, and Lionel Giles. *Sun Tzŭ on the Art of War, the Oldest Military Treatise in the World*. London: Luzac & Co., 1910.

"The Technology of the Great Zhou Dynasty." Google Sites. Accessed December 05, 2016. https://sites.google.com/a/brvgs. k12.va.us/zhoutechnologyproject/.

Tzu, Sun. "Sun Wu and His Book: Introduction." *The Art of War*. Accessed December 05, 2016. http://www.online-literature. com/suntzu/artofwar/0/.

Ye, Lang, Zhenggang Fei, and Tianyou Wang. *China: Five Thousand Years of History and Civilization*. Hong Kong: City University of Hong Kong Press, 2007.

Yuan, Haiwang, Ronald G. Knapp, Margot E. Landman, and Gregory Veeck, eds. *This Is China: The First 5,000 Years*. Great Barrington, MA: Berkshire Publishing Group, 2010.

Zong, Fubang, and Shinao Chen. *Zuo Zhuan*. Tai Bei Shi: Jin Xiu, 1992.

INDEX

Page numbers in **boldface** are illustrations. Entries in **boldface** are glossary terms.

ABOUT THE AUTHOR

MEGHAN COOPER is a mother and educator living in Brooklyn, NY.